NOT GHOSTS, BUT SPIRITS

VOLUME III

Querencia Press, LLC
Chicago Illinois

QUERENCIA PRESS

ISBN 978 1 959118 57 2

www.querenciapress.com

First Published in 2023

Querencia Press, LLC
Chicago IL

Printed & Bound in the United States of America

CONTENTS

Scene Select – Ambyunderock (they/them)

We move place to place,
Nomadic by nature even within a tiny space,
Scene to scene sometimes not being seen,
In a car we pass scenes created and amassed near and far,
How often do we reflect as the scenes pass?,
Do we contemplate as we wait?,
Even the mere second we pass by trying not to be late,
Give our brain time to elaborate,
Take a second more and you will see the plethora that is in store.

Bimini Bon-Boulash Perched Atop the Tower of London – Alex Carrigan (he/him)

People that use the British flag as
a symbol for their intolerable views
must forget what the 'union' Jack stood for.
My England is for everyone.
What does patriotism meant to you?
I wanna be inside EU.

I remember being attacked by
a group of football fans
for being visibly queer.
I was told I would make their children gay.
I hope the person's kids are gay
and I hope they're happy.

The last 18 months since the show
have been incredible, but I've encountered
so many snakes.
I've been sued, lied to, heartbroken
by people I thought were my friends.
People are fine with you until you start to succeed.

Grateful for my life and everything I get to do,
but it has come at a price. I'm in a place where
I'm happy now, but this year I have been
the unhappiest I've ever been.
I'm done with the fake people.
I'm gonna continue to do what I do,
and if you're real, then I'll fuck with you.

Hey, @MayorofLondon...
remember endorsing me as your successor?
Let's get the Tories out completely and
then get a plan in motion.
It's the era of embellishments, clashing,
and maximalism, baby
Ready when you are!

Hahaha, love pissing people off.
Still I rise, and I'm just getting started.

Source: @biminibabes

The Vivienne Does a Tip Spot Outside 10 Downing Street – Alex Carrigan (he/him)

Pro tip: read through the script before choosing roles.
New Prime Minister.
Ugh, why can't somebody cool do it for a change?
So sick of boring, 15 denier-wearing,
beige faced, never-left-London morons
running this country.

Can't Joanna Lumley do it?
We've had enough clowns, thanks!
Wish they'd throw mash potato over Boris.

If you're gonna do a character,
do a character,
not something similar/"this will do."
Commit to your craft.

I'm howling at some of the comments!
I'm a "deviant!"
"Pushing an agenda!"
"Don't let the kids watch!"
"I'll never watch again!"

Well, in the meantime,
turn off *Mrs. Doubtfire*, *White Chicks*,
Mrs. Brown's Boys, and Lily Savage.
Don't go see *Matilda the Musical*.

I'm literally a man in a frock.
An unapologetic masterclass on how to live life!
What's real is people, conversations, laughter, and theatre.
Even if you're doing your own version,
there should be a standard and not laziness.

Oh, this isn't aimed at anyone in particular.
I just see so many performers that do shit half-assed,
when I know what they're earning.
It's so sloppy.
Oh gal, the burns, the glues,
the blisters, if they only knew.
Lol, if you scroll enough you'll see plenty of it!

And who even cares?
Season's been and gone.
I'm off for a Sicilian cappuccino!
Hope I can find one.

Source: @THEVIVIENNEUK

Blu Hydrangea Reveals Her Rusted Nail – Alex Carrigan (he/him)

Yesterday, I posted a hate message I received,
and someone replied 'keep your chins up.'

Thank you, love.

You'd be unbearable if you got on
that show for more than a few seconds.

Don't take out your age insecurities on me.
We see your negative comments, so be nice.
The people you may have 'lost' as fans,
you probably didn't want in the first place!!!!

They should have an option to hide subscribed blue ticks.

When you meet a queen who uses Facetune, they look different.
But, when you meet a queen who uses FaceApp...
who did this photo even start off as?

Wait, you're being nice?
Oh, was this a compliment?
Sometimes, I just come to
the comment section with my guard up.
I did feel really pretty.

I mean, I'm also incredible at what I do,
but I do love drag and intake it in any form I can.
Drag Race has given me the opportunity
to buy a house before I'm 30.
I'm ok, babe.

I'm sorry, Crystal.
Idk how my dildo got on your set.
It's such a Northern Irish thing;
do a shot every time she does it.

Sorry I was steaming.
I'm a little drunk,
and this was a sensory overload.

*Source: @BluHydrangea_*

Silky Nutmeg Ganache Hijacks the Airwaves – Alex Carrigan (he/him)

Are y'all not accustomed to black, queer people?
Y'all used TS Madison quotes
but didn't know who she was.

Y'all defending bullshit.
My black ass never said anything that crazy
to a queen on Season 11,
yet I was met with death threats.
The block thumb is strong today.

I have to go the extra mile and
other girls don't even have to go an inch????
Answer that. But answer with truth.

I love how whiteness is always supported.
Cry and the white fans will forgive.

Since so many of y'all are unbiased
and you don't see color,
the next time a black queen
reads a white girl,
be sure to say it's her unique humor,
she's making good tv,
or you just don't understand her.

I'm just a BIPOC that felt that jab.
But I'm used to it.
White queens, you can take BLM
off your name now,
the trend is over.

Today has been stressful.
I need wine and chorizo.
In that order.

We all got on *Drag Race* to
simply make our family proud
and create a new life for ourselves.

No matter how the fandom may react to us,
I'm sure every girl in all 14 seasons
wanted the same.
Give my sister her flowers.

Source: @SilkyGanache

**This selection of 4 poems first appeared in*
Now Let's Get Brunch: A Collection of RuPaul's Drag Race Twitter Poetry by Alex Carrigan

Untitled – Irina Tall (she/her)

It's a Wonderful Life – Helen Coats (she/they)

CW: mention of child death, COVID-19, childhood bullying, cisheteronormativity

Strange, to play yourself and the angel
who announces your death.

Bedford Falls—all its inhabitants cozied up
into boxes on a screen, their years spun

out live on YouTube, every townsperson
played by the same six actors, every actor

eager to get back onstage but glad to be
here, with PDF scripts at their fingertips.

You play Harry Bailey, hotshot pilot, and
Ernie the taxi driver and Joe the salesman

and Mr. Potter's goon with the glasses.
For Harry Bailey, brother to George,

you wear the tuxedo you borrowed
from a man whose shoulders are broader

than your slim narrow Coats' slopes.
And yes, it doesn't really fit you, but it also

becomes you. And then
you play Clarence—genderless,

sweet angel, waking George by your grave:
Harry Bailey / fell through the ice /

and was drowned at the age of nine.
When *you* were nine, the boy who stole

the lamb you brought to show and tell
at your artsy homeschool daycamp

hid it in the bathroom. You cried
outside, couldn't go in because

you'd get in trouble again, just like back
in preschool when you said that there

wasn't any problem with kissing girls
like the boys did and you ran around

trying to kiss them while they squealed
and ran away. But that was Pottersville.

In Bedford Falls, Harry Bailey is grown
and flying someone else's F6F Hellcat

through a blizzard to reach his brother.
No canopy over the cockpit—wind, skin.

He is not frozen—your limbs are warm.
His heart is beating, and you are young.

**In December 2020, I was cast in a long-distance Zoom production of* It's a Wonderful Life *and played several genderbent characters. It provided a great source of community in the face of isolation and helped me discover that I am genderqueer.*

Why do I write about being bi? – Helen Coats (she/they)

after "Diving into the Wreck" by Adrienne Rich & Zami: A New Spelling of My Name by Audre Lorde

CW: mild body horror, implied religious trauma

Is it to scratch / an itch / like I scratch / the eczema marbled
down my legs / like poison ivy's tattooed cousin / always

permanent / like the South Carolina-shaped scab / under
my left eye / that crinkles / blood / when I cut / too far /

with the nails / that I never clean / like my car / with the
Starbucks cup / black with mold / around the lip / still

simmering / by the passenger's side?
I travel the similes down / until I forget / where I started.

And I need the (/) because otherwise / I will not stop /
when / and where / I need to. / I will not rest. / What a mess—

my skin / always red / always scabbed / always unwelcome
on my soul / has been since I was a kid / and I have to believe /

that souls / or spirits / or something holy / exists /
because I need / something / other / than this / big / rust / ooze.

I think / (but I am not sure) / that I write about being bi /
to catch a throughline. / A train line.

The 5 o'clock / from itching and peeling / back to when my body /
didn't shed so much / and I didn't mind /

that I was / (and am still) / allergic to grass. / I lay out /
in its green / in the lunch break light / and loved the blue /

in my friend's blue jeans / not washed-out denim
but a blue that / *pops*— party balloon / blue.

I played / with her beach-sun curls / and didn't realize /
that maybe us joking around / that the grass was like /

the sea / and the bugs were like octopi / (a wolf spider /
was the kraken) / and we were mermaids / diving /

into the wreck / would develop into / a memory /
of an afternoon / that I would lock in my dark room /

for years / until one day / I would read Adrienne Rich /
and remember the octopi / and open the door.

I am ready to return / to sing the praises /
of her gold hair / and the irregular blue / of her jeans /

and / like Audre Lorde / come home to history /,
breathing to the pace / of a joy / I was meant for.

Drought Summer – Helen Coats (she/they)

CW: homophobia, rejection after coming out

My coming-out letter bore seeds
you refused to plant—
the ballerinas I watched
arch and bend
to Gymnopédie No. 1.

Three girls, arms long and
soft and open, forming
a teardrop triquetra.

It was high school and I
did not know what my eyes
were doing, who I wanted—

I just knew that I was struck,
my lungs achingly shuttered,
and I wandered home alone,
bruised by the memory
of thirty candlewick fingers
reaching out, six sets of eyelashes,
winter-frosted ferns under stage lights,
three scallops, three leotard-bound chests.

I thought of joining them.
Imagined them pulling together,
arm crossed over arm, forming rank—
les petites cygnes, without a fourth.
Their heads, their long necks turned away.

I thought of seashells
smashed to grit and moth wings
melting to ash and other small, lost,
delicate things I dared not touch.

My letter bore these seeds
and you refused to plant them.
I expected that.
I prepared for it.

I knew you wouldn't bury them
in the soil with the beautiful,
dirt-lined hands that have kneaded
migraines from my shoulders
so many times. I thought
if I read you that letter,
it would become a terrarium
and I could grow the seeds myself.

I didn't know that I would walk
into the sun room for breakfast
the next day—the room that is not
really a patio but not really just a room,
with windows on all sides,
pale light sifting through the hair
of your summer ferns so that
everything is green and new
with the arrival of morning—

and you would not look at me.
You would not speak to me.
I ate two bites of Shredded Wheat
and then you left my alone.

The walls of my terrarium
began to shrink. And the soil,
to crack like my eczema skin.
Drought summer.

On the first Forgiveness Sunday after I admitted to myself that I was no longer an Orthodox Christian – Helen Coats (she/they)

CW: religious trauma, parental struggle

When I couldn't forgive the woman with the smile like mine
and the man with the hair and blue-rimmed eyes like mine

my friend asked: What version of them do you want?
Who do you want them to be?

It would be easier if they were the little glass elephants
you sometimes find in gas stations with "you break it,

you buy it" printed in Comic Sans, taped to the shelves.
I wish there was some cold transaction I could figure

instead of the *yes, and*
I'm doing now, I'm tired of *yes, and*ing

but still there is your smile like mine
and your hair and blue-rimmed eyes like mine

and my ribs are gnawing to drag me back through the dirt
to you. I read the texts you send on Forgiveness Sunday—

Helen, forgive us sinners for any way
we have offended you...and the word

offended rots like chicken that the least favorite roommate
cooked and decided not to throw away until

too late and so now its ghost
wanders freakish in the kitchen.

Mormon Prom – Helen Coats (she/they)

CW: implied religious trauma, cisheteronormativity

Have you heard of anything as queer-coded as a bunch of
Mormon kids and me riding in a big white van to Mormon prom,
screaming [Sunday clean] Broadway showtunes, our lungs at
Everest volume, and boogie-ing in our seats like it's 1978?

My friend and I used to sit together at lunch in Ms. Jackson's
tutoring center, editing Google docs with all the memes and
Marvel fanfic we could fit on a single page. And then we had
French together, where we kept putting squirrels in boxes 'cuz
the words "écureuil" and "boîte" sounded funny. She
called me up and asked me to prom 'cuz she was the only
single Mormon in her friend group and I [non-Mormon me],
like to dance 'cuz I'm a [redacted] theater kid.

We matched corsages. White flowers, white dresses with black
sweaters over spaghetti straps to cover shoulders. The two of us,
shoulderless. Her medical tag explaining that she has epilepsy, a
silver bracelet. Her insulin pump tucked beneath her dress. A
promise from me to her anxious mother that if anything happened
I would take care of her daughter. I only made the promise
'cuz we knew she would worry otherwise. We were not worried.
We were going to party hard, and by hard, I mean
we were going to eat an irresponsible amount of Oreos.

Dinner at a kid's parents' home first, and they all called the kid's
mom "Sister" something, and the couples took pics out on the porch
and my friend and I took a pic too. The petals on our corsages
browned a little on the edges but we did not want to take them off.

And then, the crammed white van to Mormon prom. My friend
beside me, arm pressed to arm, her body heat making me sweat
before we ever hit the dance floor.

The guys who danced with me did their best to convert me.
They kept asking me if I wanted to settle down with anyone
some day. I said I didn't know. The idea frightened me.
My friend started feeling tired and went out on the porch
for some air and apple juice and insulin. I went with her.

The porch, damp and brown patio boards mottled with mold.
The night, indigo. So different from the golden fairy lights transforming the barn behind, the distant bass bump from the DJ playing [Sunday clean] songs, the whoops and cheers from the other kids that had taken on a dreamlike filter.
They were far away.

We didn't talk about anything significant. First Avengers movie coming out, how much we love the obviously straight, cisgender Loki. How happy I was for the invitation, how glad my friend was to have me come along, so glad that she was not alone.
Yes, I agreed, so good not to be alone.

unsolicited feedback – johanna monson geerts (she/her)

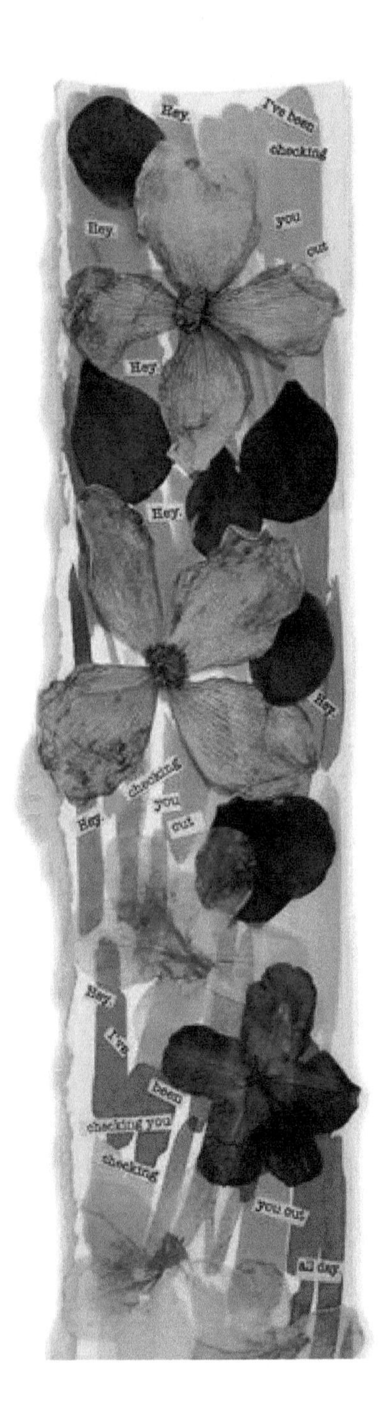

A Cork In Both Wrists – Jake Price (he/him)

The boy with violet blood

likes to bleed

because that is the only time anyone loves him.

Some people pour wine slowly,

    letting it steep,

    letting it aerate.

Some people just want to get tipsy over pasta.

If the boy bled into a glass

    all the vineyards would go belly up,

    the grape vine banisters lining the ivory staircase wither into dust,

liquor store owners smash their bottles outside their shops

and leave red stains on the sidewalks.

The difference between getting drunk and blacking out:

    you remember drinking from someone's wrist

    or you don't.

All that's left in the boy is spirits.

From violet blood to vodka.

to the person who taught me how to think in cursive, I'm sorry I miss you – Jake Price (he/him)

A garden full of daylilies,
only daylilies.

/

I water them with ice sculptures I leave to melt inside the greenhouse.
I like to think the flowers see a metaphor in it,
and are not just sitting there with their petal tongues hanging,
waiting for a drip,
a drop of meaning.

/

After they bloom, I dehead them like you're supposed to,
so they can blossom again in the fall.

/

I showed you the garden once, and the stream behind it,
and the field between the garden and the stream,
and the foxglove that grew along the side of the greenhouse,
and I melted in front of the daylilies, their petal tongues hanging,
waiting for a drip,
a drop of meaning.

Pop! – Jake Price (he/him)

ACT #1: The Numbers

Marcus died while behind the wheel of an eighteen-wheeler going sixty-six miles per hour. After driving for a full twenty-four hours at that point, the nineteen crushed Styrofoam coffee cups and three Red Bull Cans rattled as they shifted behind the driver's seat. His heart exploded inside of his chest. Slumped forward on the steering wheel, he merged lanes and jerked the truck back in between the lines on the highway. "Keep it between the mustard and mayonnaise" as his uncle had told him when he first learned to drive. His last thought.

He had been late to a drop off and needed to get his inventory to the distribution center by 3:00 PM that day. He died at noon, his least favorite time to drive. The west Texas sun always made the asphalt so hot it started to melt his tires. He hated the smell. The trucking company that Marcus worked for, *Challenger Transport,* paid him forty cents for every mile he drove. After death, he made twenty-five cents before his truck plowed into the back of an SUV. A family of five turned into a family of three, with a three hundred grand medical bill, two funerals, and one divorce filing.

-

ACT #2: The Best Family Road Trip In The History of Family Road Trips

"STOP KICKING ME—"

"Don't kick your sister, Jeffery. We're supposed to be having fun."

"Livin' easy, Lovin' free, Season ticket on a one-way ride"

"Who can have fun going camping? Why are we—"

"Honey, don't—"

"Who wants to spend the weekend in the woods?"

"Goin' down, Party time, My friends are gonna be there too, yeah"

"I am excited for it."

"Thank you, Sarah."

"Shut up, Sarah."

"Like a wheel, Gonna spin it, Nobody's gonna mess me around"

"That is enough! I am sick of your attitude young man—"

"Your mother is right, Jeffery. Do I need to pull over?"

"Hey momma, Look at me, I'm on my way to the Promised Land, ow"

"Why don't we play a game Mr. Grumpy Pants?"

"The animal guessing game?"

"Sure, I'll go first."

"I'm on the highway to hell, On the highway to hell"

"Can I play?

"No, only—"

"Of course you can Sarah."

"Okay, does it live in the water?"

"No."

"Does it—"

ACT #3: ***Martha***

The breeze that came in through the window was a gift from God. It made the curtains turn into sails and the setting sunlight made everything feel more holy. The air conditioner had stopped working the previous afternoon, and Martha was grateful for the reprieve. Two box fans circulated hot, stuffy air throughout the apartment, and there she sat on the living room couch, sweating. The TV was playing reruns of a show she didn't know the name of, and she didn't have to. She was only watching it with her eyes; her mind was elsewhere. As it had been. It was impossible to be present in the heat.

She couldn't stop thinking about the argument. The way her husband had slammed his palms on their kitchen table.

"What do you want me to do, Martha? I don't understand. You complain cause we're poor, so I go and work my ass off. Then you complain because I am away working my ass—"

"That's not what this is Marcus, you know that. Don't act like you're out there sweating under the sun. You drive truck. There is a fucking air conditioner blasting in your face all hours of the day."

He had stared at her. A mug of coffee steamed in front of both of them. Untouched. After a ten count, he answered. "What do you want me to do, Martha?"

"I want you too..." She caught herself laughing for the first time in a year. "I want you to have a life again. I want you to be. You're not Marcus anymore, you know that right? You're a robot. You have wires in your chest and oil in your joints and you need to be plugged into an outlet—"

"WHAT DOES THAT MEAN MARTHA?"

That was two days ago. He had left that night. He had to drive across the state into new Mexico for a drop off. The air conditioner had broken the day after and Martha had called him once it had stopped rattling its last breaths. He hadn't answered. So, she sat and watched reruns and sweat, letting her mind replay the argument over in her mind. She remembered it fondly. That was the first fight they had had since college, and she thought they finally had hope. Something to hold on to. Couples that made it work fought. It's the ones that didn't that ended up splitting.

The phone rang in the kitchen. She let it ring twice before she stood, feeling the cool breeze from the window on her skin. Rounding the couch, the floor changed from carpet to tile underneath her bare feet.

"Hello?"

Transition Goals – Zephyr James (they/them)

The day that I injected testosterone into my body for the first time, I lit candles with a whispered prayer to my future Self and laid out each medical supply like an offering. Soon after, a rainbow bandage adorned my thigh—a visual reminder of my devotion to Self. In this quiet moment, I began the process of making myself whole.

And yet, the predominant expectation is that I must be rejecting a part of myself to transition. The price to be taken seriously is a perverse mandate that I must be ashamed of my own femininity; that I must discard it or treat it like an intruder in my home. People presume to know my experience better than I do myself, and false narratives are foisted on me with stunning ease—it is assumed that I am either a 'man trapped in the wrong body' or a dangerously confused woman.

In clinical and social settings, I've been interrogated about my "transition goals." I am expected to provide a list of desired aesthetic changes and to detail my dysphoria in ways that make sense to cisgender people, or to binary trans people. "Acceptance" too often comes in the form of being treated like a trans man. At every turn, I'm forced to choose a box. I am othered or erased daily. But I refuse to accept pathologizing or pity from those who are threatened by my unshackling.

Most people cannot fathom that love—not hatred or disgust—is the core of my transness.

Do you hear me when I say that my full trans Self came forward *after* I healed my trauma? Does it make you uneasy to know that this is the pinnacle of sanity, rather than a punishment or illness trailing behind my string of personal atrocities? What if I told you that my journey through gender has been a spiritual reconciliation?

I don't reject myself. I don't disown my femininity, or my lived experience as a woman. Yes, there are parts of me being shed—parts of me that I love and honor. But those parts were masks and coping mechanisms. Fierce and strong and beautiful, but an illusion. *Those* are the parts that were forged in hell, not the parts coming forward now.

You want to know my deepest transition goal? You want to know why I would mutilate myself to be visible in my trans body? My embodied trans self after medical transition will be an internal place of unity and an external challenge to systems that dehumanize us all.

Why is it more comfortable for you to talk about what's in my pants than what's in my soul?

Bodies on Display – Shannon Clem (she/they)

Eyes loiter bashful
inside a gymnasium
locker room.

Hiccupping thighs
strut by; vie for attention
from fellow women
in lieu of dicey men.

God's head turned,
86ed from the shower—
Its head beating down on
hypertrophic scars—

Future tattoos.
Uncomfortable nudes
screaming,
"Look here, now! I dare you!"

Glare-check my forehead.
Make sure there is no fever.
No raised lines to transcribe
this body's Braille:

Secrets—Idents.
Shame—Requisite.
Feminine—Ecstasy.

A Girl Inside – Shannon Clem (she/they)

A vintage brick-red heel
with cutouts in the toes—
Like the decorated body
of a little hollowed guitar,
rests on my memory:

Underneath,
my nails painted pink—
Wet and wild, just like her.
Hiding—
A girl inside, a girl inside—
A girl.

One crooked step
and the guitar's neck broke.
Underneath,
my nails sticking out—
Toes trying to breathe
without inducing blood.

She slips off her flip-flops—
Barefoot, like naked.
Offering in chivalry,
the shoes off her feet
as though they were rings
and her hand.

I thank her
in cheeks pink with flush—
Step affirmative rhythms
with open toes.
Exposed—
A girl outside, a girl outside—
A girl.

Things She Can't Live Without – Shannon Clem (she/they)

"Heavy Metal / Head in the Sand / Hidden Depths / Burning Demand / The Things She Can't Live Without"

Crabapples – Marissa Wolfe (she/her)

The mother hunched over the washing machine, phantom blow dealt to her insides. White and gray blurred within her watery vision and through autopilot effort the laundry basket in her hands had been set gently on the ground. A trembling hand clutched the straight edge of the appliance as she lowered to her knees, a prayer-pose for divinity, corrupted. Her hands fell limply into her lap and she rested her forehead on the front of the machine, metal shifting beneath the weight of her skull. Her ankles began to ache, overextended, unnatural in their positioning. She could not move. She would not move. This is where she wanted to be. Where she needed to be. Where she deserved to be.

There was only pain where there should be pleasure. A cold sense of transaction, of chaotic callings guised in latex and lace, conquered flowery warmth. Love was conditional, apparently, but devotion was not. She'd cracked her shell, realizing the beauty in her softness, but her hardened exterior was scattered across the floor and cut her feet with frustrating regularity. Her tenderness was not a gift, but a fee—a price to pay for the life she'd chosen to lead.

She could not maintain her pose and rolled over, back against the machine. The tears were hysterical now. Sticky mucus clogged her nose and mixed with the rivers flowing down her gasping lips. Her head rolled to the side and a memory projected onto the sagging walls of the laundry room.

She was seven and had picked handfuls of crabapples from the tree in the front yard. She stowed them beneath the rusted lid of a tiny charcoal grill kept underneath the house. When her grandfather discovered what she'd been doing, he'd scolded her. She'd burst into tears and ran sobbing into the house. She recalled the obvious shock on Papa's face as he realized that this was not about apples. He sent her mother in to talk with her as she cried bitterly in her room. They spoke of the neighborhood boy who'd visited that day and took a piece of her around the corner and down the hill. She felt pulled, roped in by the need for his attention and the desire to give him what he wanted. But attention had come and gone, and the seven-year-old was drained, guilty for reasons she did not understand. In the most tender of tones, her mother told the little girl that she needed to learn to say no. He was a grade older than her, and despite the lewd gestures he'd make in her peripherals, she would never meet his eyes in the hallway again.

A montage of groping hands and lingering eyes filled her mind. She was nearly thirty and had been emptied too many times over. If it was not sex that was demanded of her, it was attention. If not attention, ability. Even the pursuit of art and knowledge were not sacred acts. She yearned for innocence, for simplicity. For gentle, tender, worshipping touch void of entitled wandering. To submit as an act of devotion, not expectation. She wanted to feel curious and clean; to know anticipation instead of dread. Had these sweeter moments completely slipped between her fingers or was there still a chance for her to grasp the remnants of those fleeting days? Could she still find rosy evenings, nights where the only intrusiveness to be found was the touch of a winter chill within the lofty breezes of early spring?

Papa died seven years prior. Her childhood home had cracks in the foundation and leaked when it rained. The crabapple tree dwindled with disease, but there was a dip in the ground where it once stood. She'd twisted her ankle in it more times than she could count, reminded of its existence as she limped to the porch to tend to her swelling joint. She'd withered, dried, and grown anew, an outwardly unshakeable perennial rooted in rocky, unforgiving clay but each bloom seemed to yield less than the season before. Within a mature, fertile body, a waify child cried beneath the shade of the crabapple tree, mourning what could not be changed and cursing all she'd done to wound herself further.

Heavy footsteps descended into the basement and walked into every room except the one the mother sat in. She almost wanted to be discovered, crouched and blubbering on the cement floor, to be found in scary, disturbing ways so that the depths of her were seen and not just discussed—gone over at the tail end of tired arguments that were never really about who or what they seemed to be about. Fate struck. Steel-toed boots ascended the creaking steps, and the mother was left there with her thoughts, staring into the vibrant eyes and goofy, ignorant grin of a stuffed animal her daughter had forgotten downstairs.

The child would be waking soon, and the mother's duties usurped her crisis, just as they always had. She wiped her nose on the collar of her tattered laundry-day shirt and rose to her feet. She picked up the basket beside her on the floor and dumped her intimates into the basin, careful to avoid pressure on her restless, protruding belly.

Overpriced, dye-free, non-toxic detergent. Delicate cycle. Water as cold as it could be. Cleanliness was an exhaustive act.

When you forget your Place – Samar Johnson (they/them)

Black Femme,

Why do you cover your mouth when you laugh or cry?
Who taught you to mute your emotional experiences?
You are not a bridled animal

Unleash

Unfurl

Swallow those that try to eat you whole
Bones and all

Goddess in Repose – Maegen McAuliffe O'Leary (she/her)

I think I'll lie down
and have a nap.

Let the earth pile over me
while it twirls on its axis.

Let the worms tunnel into me
while I snore contentedly.

Let the rain patter fearlessly
while bugs snuggle in my ear.

No, I'm not dead.
I'm resting.

Nothing to see here—
just another woman

tired of being pulled
and pinched

and pushed
and poked

and played
and prosecuted.

Just another woman
who'd rather kiss dirt

than keep listening
to this bullshit.

Yes, I think I'll have a nap.
Wake me in time

for the revolution.
I'll bring the grenades.

Pro-Choice – Maegen McAuliffe O'Leary (she/her)

In a world designed to cut us
into paper dolls,
I choose to be ravenously dimensional.

When my head
is full of raucous sounds,
I choose to sing up my throat.

When they trim, inch by inch,
the fat from our soft underside,
I choose the wick and the match

and light that motherfucker
for everyone crawling
through the dark behind me.

I choose to be a woman.

Portrait of (A) Self – Sadee Bee (she/they)

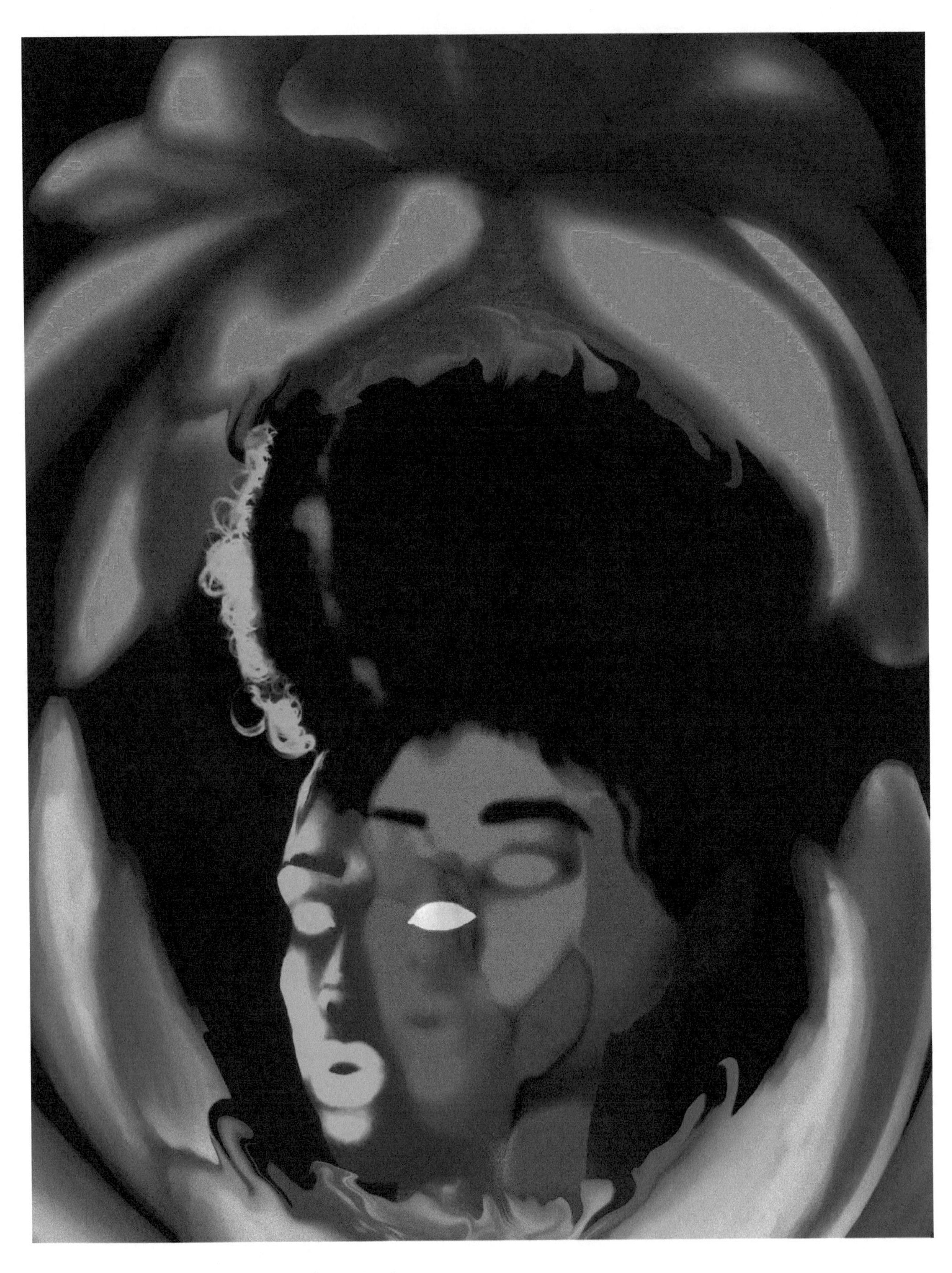

Negative Bloom – Sadee Bee (she/they)

Grip – Sadee Bee (she/they)

Wish – Anna Kohlweis (she/they)

come to my party
I have a pitch black forest road
rustling leaves
a twig that snaps.

I wish the plague was over and I found a splinter in my left heel
indistinguishable from a glimmer of hope
or a similarly small but sharp form of love.
I wish waking was tied to a soft shoulder and a scenic route ahead
our sixteen eyes in unison, looking, weaving.

I wish there was a fire in danger of dying
embers to blow into, bellows to fill
something strange, yet untroubled about the moon.
I wish blankets were so large, our curiosity about where they end bordered on concern.
I wish there was time to lie down
years pressed to the ground.

I wish for time to get lost in tenses
I wish for the kinds of friendships
in which we sew the buttons onto each other's clothes
and walk in tangled paths built on the unshakable desire
to breathe life into each other
constantly
vigorously
colliding
with care.

I wish tomorrow was a sapling
digging its roots deep into the earth
cracking open the night
inching forward
following the sound of voices
shifts in temperature
to where we sit
laughing.

Birthday – Anna Kohlweis (she/they)

I was born during a heat wave
I have been sweat for 37 years
I am an onion
I peel me forever
and you cut
and you cry
and I cry
we all cry
what a fabulous asymmetric soup I have been
since that first last day of June
what a fabulous factory of need and want
driven by its uninhabited poles
what a fabulous history of escapes.

it cools down just as it turns midnight
get up, lock the factory in a frenzy
dance to the sound of sharpening knives
sweat up a storm.
I am onion juices, glue, thumbtacks, and soft soles
everything sticks to me
I was born during a heat wave
I have been sweat for 37 years.

Permafrost – Anna Kohlweis (she/they)

do unfurl in spite of the cold
pinch the soles of my feet
in thirty-eight rows
with nails I have grown from these fingers
while hammered
need a better grasp on the ice
will shape these feet into grippers
a brittle
numbing
slippery slope
I am the mother, the son, the unholy, the most
cryogenically frozen love potion
preserved in permafrost
for future generations
lusting for scraps and glimmer
see it all wash down the falls
these precious hopes, shaken up
naked, bubbly
they plummet

stripped down

cracked open

hungry.

Theft – Anna Kohlweis (she/they)

while you speak
I tie my shoe laces
maybe you notice
the extra knots for safety

how urgently I need to climb down
the spiral staircase of your chest
into your damp, dark, mold-ridden base
meant to say:
with my Swiss army knife i need to go
where you grow your heart fungi puffball
bitter oyster
death cap
morel
and when you look the other way
I cut a few of them
scarf them down raw
until my throat tightens.

Instead of Banning Assault Weapons – Subhaga Crystal Bacon (she/they)

—An Erasure from "Everything That Happened in Anti-Trans Legislation This Week: April 2-9," Them

Arkansas

gives the right to

refuse gender-affirming

restroom, bathroom, locker room, or shower room

sexual

indecency

Idaho ban

s puberty blockers, surgeries, hormone replacement

allows "corrective" procedures

restrict s materials for minors schools,

libraries.

Indiana under-18 gender-affirming

health ban.

Kansas

"women's rights" defines gender as

sex at birth.

sports ban bill, is now law.

genital inspections.

North Dakota this week.

ten anti-trans bills progressed in one day.-

a forced misgendering

birth

certificate bans non-binary gender

For Brianna Ghey – Subhaga Crystal Bacon (she/they)

—It is the exception that interests the devil – Sylvia Plath

To become a schoolgirl wearing a skirt and blazer
white shirt and tie. To grow out your hair, tie it back
let it fall. To document yourself, a blossoming to share
on *TikTok*. To sit on a bench on a Saturday in the winter
sun, or eating a snack, smiling at the one behind the camera,
as captured in the picture in the newspaper after your death.

To find yourself inside the body in which you were born,
a cocoon containing a different truth. To know yourself
as more than the sum of your parts. Your youth. Your spark.
To dare to live a different life, break free from biology.
For this, you are exceptional: stabbed by two teenagers
in a park: *targeted. No evidence to suggest hate* in your death.

Locked Doors – Subhaga Crystal Bacon (she/they)

See the car traveling the highway,
driven by a beloved professor,
full of theater students coming back
from another college performance.

1976, the Bicentennial, the year
I finally came out to myself—
that summer—after kissing a girl.
But this was before, winter.

A trip to—maybe—Shippensburg
where we went often to debate
and declaim poetry, a restaurant
with a *groaning board* where we'd

gorge ourselves on delicacies
like white asparagus. Drink scotch
at the hotel where we shared beds,
four to a room. The shaping hands

we lay upon each other, not sexual
but intimate, friends. I was lost.
Looking back now, I see myself
a hot wire flailing but still failing

to make a spark. I was a desire
unfulfilled because unnamable.
Driving home on Sunday—day most
prime for death to me—a blank space

in a week of doing, I fell into darkness
unspoken—unnamable—and pulled
the handle on the car door, wanting
the fall, the pain of landing on asphalt

sixty miles an hour. But no; the door
was locked. Still, the sound it made,
a click that met obstruction, shocked
us all awake. Nothing was said.

We rode the rest of the way in the dark
and came first to my parents' house
where I lived—the others in dorms
in town. As I walked away from the car

in a chorus they shouted *We love you,*
Crystal. My mother at the door
scandalized. *What on earth!* she said.
Not one for grand gestures. Not one

to know how much I wanted to be dead.

Venus Dreaming – Subhaga Crystal Bacon (she/they)

It's still pleasing to my eye, this aging sack of pain.
Still rosy, stained with ink winding up my arms,
a fading story etched in skin. Shoulder-cup bear,
lotus, snake of Sanskrit twined in leaves. The Great Wave
splashing over a form of my name *Om Subhagayai*
Namaha, invoking the Divine. The Mother.

I gaze and gaze like Narcissus in his pool. Lovely boy,
so lovely, a flower, perhaps a fool. I, too, am lovely.
Hair pulled back, my face unlined. I am neither mother,
nor boy. I wear this body: breasts meeting belly
rounded under ribs. This mound of Venus dreaming.
I'm not a flower, not transformed by my own gaze,
the reflecting pool broken by the crashing wave.

I Carry Your Heart With Me – R.S. Kendle (she/they)

After you discarded it
Cast it aside
With your coat, your whisky, your body.

A crumpled heap
To be cleared out
Alongside yesterday's snow.

I gathered it up
Cupped it carefully in my hands
The way you do a baby bird.

I slipped it in my own chest
Stretched the cavity
To make room for you.

It felt strange at first
Feeling the flutters of a heartbeat
Slowly coming back to life.

But over time we got used to each other
A duet of lover and beloved.
Co-dependent.

Your heart grew
Resilient
Strengthened over the cracks.

Whilst mine wilted
Tired from caring for you
Harbouring this ravening passenger.

I carried you through a decade
Through stasis and reverence.
Through convalescence.

Then I realised I had outgrown you,
Outgrown your memory.
I had to cast you out.

And in that night: an ode to sisterhood – Kaylee Hernandez (she/they)

We saw a hare cross   our   path
A cricket jumped across the ground
Where we shared our hearts
                                                                Open

Near the Rio Grande
By the Border town
Where we all grew up
Where we still live

Our hearts poured together
Into a beaker of love
Elements combined perfectly—
A chemical reaction
We all cheered for

I laid on the tile
Swatting mosquitos
Even though it's October
I tried to wear a long sleeve
I knew it was still too hot
But we walked together
Like it was colder
                              And nicer
And like we lived somewhere else
Somewhere we could go walking
                                                                for miles

Sometimes I think our souls met long ago
On a different plane
4 sisters
4 bloods running through veins
One love uniting
We belong together
Never to part
In a place that holds importance to each of us
In different ways
In this place of palm trees and tears by the river

Sunny Days Ahead – Kaylee Hernandez (she/they)

Digital Collage
11.5x14
2021

La Guera – Kaylee Hernandez (she/they)

My hair is light and my skin is pale
But that does not mean I'm not one of you.
That does not mean I don't enjoy the pachangas en la noche
And I don't eat la salsa verde que me hace llorar y dice 'Ay, que rico!"

You might look at me and think I don't belong
"Ay, una guera que no sabe nada."
But this is my home.
I can't imagine belonging anywhere other than the land of cerveza y pan.
Esta es mi tierra tambien porque soy de Brownsville.

I am here, too.

You might look at me and see someone who looks like she belongs in Canada or Ohio, but I cannot imagine belonging anywhere else.
I belong to my land of dos mundos y dos tierras.
I belong to rice and beans and tortillas de harina.
I belong to a place that has no predictable weather for any given hour

But you can bet on the palm trees swaying in the wind,
The bougainvilleas blooming in the spring
The tide coming and going; my constant in many a storm.
The climate may not be predictable, but I have come to love it anyway,
this climate of thrashing thunderstorms and catastrophic hurricanes,
calm seas and sunny days.

When you hear my last name and you see a picture of my dad
with his piel moreno y bigote grande
you are confused.
Believe me, I've been confused my whole life.
I don't look like I belong. A lot of days I can feel it, too.
Acceptance is hardly an easy task.
But I have come to belong to this place of miel y leche...or rather pan y cerveza...
My hair is light and my skin is pale
But that does not mean I don't belong here.

Border Princess – Kaylee Hernandez (she/they)

Digital Collage
11.5x14
2021

Corte de Pelo – Kaylee Hernandez (she/they)

Scissors blind me for a second, gleaming in the fluorescent light
I close my eyes.
Romeo Santos, Pitbull & Shakira blaring behind me
I kind of hate coming here.
I sit calmly as my hair is moistened, then cut.
I can feel cold water on my neck.
Sometimes the ladies won't talk to me at all
If they do, the conversation is always the same
"Yes, this is my natural color...si, es natural"
"No, I've never dyed it...no, nunca"
"Aww, thank you so much"
"Yeah, I know it's really thick. My dad's hair is real thick, too"
Always complimented on the color—I guess a dirty blonde shade that isn't too common around here.
I've always told people it came from my mom, even though her hair is white now...

Haircuts always make me anxious—it's a pretty intimate space you share with someone you don't know for longer than a bank line conversation
Maybe it feels so intimate because someone is touching your head and your hair.
Who else besides lovers and family, maybe children, place their hands on your head?
After all, the head is keeper of the brain, a few layers of skull, skin, and hair between others and your innermost thoughts.

I'm swiveled around to face myself in the mirror, although blurry until I replace my glasses—held tightly under the plastic chair cloth. I always feel like a ghost in a sheet until it's taken off.

Looking at myself I can see me, "a fresh 'do, a new you?"
But I feel the same.

Anxiety – Kaylee Hernandez (she/they)

Digital Collage
21X21
2023

A Day at the Beach – Charlie J. Stephens (they/them)

I thought Jude was flirting with me at the cafe, but then she started talking about how some Tibetans believe that we've all lived so many lives that everyone we pass on the street was once a mother or a father to us. Beautiful, yes. But not too sexy.

It was okay; I still had some hope regarding Jude. Even though someone in middle school (over 30 years ago now—apparently these things have a way of sticking with you) told me that my face looked like the bottom of a bucket, I was not without my charms. I tried to remember that, especially in situations like this. My older brother Victor tried to protect me from the biggest bullies, including our parents, but even he couldn't prevent the mean world from seeping in.

"Clem," he used to tell me, "You're not like other girls, but that's your superpower. Don't let them make you think they're better than you because they're not." He was always good at seeing something in me that I couldn't. He was like that with everyone.

It was my day off, so I walked along the muddy river to the ocean with my mid-morning coffee, still thinking about Jude, even though Jude probably wasn't thinking of me. I thought of Victor too, how if he was still alive he would be the person I'd most want to be with on the beach, how much he would appreciate it. The dark, evergreen trees were magnificently bored—no wind—and the water was a glass mirror reflecting everything. The gray sky sat heavy and low, and I was breathing in whole clouds. They floated around and pressed up underneath my rib cage, trying to get back out.

Near a stand of Pampas grass, two parents in winter coats and ski hats set up optimistic beach chairs in the damp air and watched their two half-naked kids run around in the sand, impervious to the cold. The children jumped in the roaring Pacific and climbed on driftwood, whipped the sky and their legs with bull kelp and threw rocks and sand at the waves and each other.

I found a battered, old log to sit on, felt the smooth wood underneath me. I watched the waves, watched the horizon, and watched the kids doing all their unpredictable kid things. The little boy was probably six and the girl maybe nine. I'd never wanted kids of my own but they are sometimes fun to watch from a distance or from behind some kind of barrier, kind of like going to the zoo. The younger one started crying and rubbing his eyes—pointing at his sister with a snarl—it was probably a handful of sand that got him.

Jude is our small town's only therapist, and though I would benefit from some help working through the old traumas I still carry around, I was holding out because of the ethical clause that therapists can't be romantically involved with their clients. There's another therapist one town over, about an hour's drive away, but he's a pinched old thing—very Freudian—so I decided to just keep trying to sort out my problems on my own.

Jude's got the strong, lean body of a forest rabbit and crooked little teeth I regularly find myself wanting to run my tongue across. She often seems a little unkempt, with her wild hair she lets fly every which way and the loose clothing she wears, like she's in disguise, hiding a secret. She lives alone above town on the bluffs, in a little blue house that's mostly windows. I've been to parties she's thrown there over the years, where we've talked and laughed so easily on varied topics most people don't have the patience for. Once, a few years ago, we even watched the sun come up together, listening to Joni Mitchell on her old record player and having so many feelings. Or at least I think we were. She comes so close, and I can feel her pull and reach and want, but she always decides to disappear in the end. It's been like this for a long time.

I'm not sure why I haven't given up on Jude. There's just something about her.

I'd been looking out at the waves, watching them crash so mightily against the cliffs, still thinking about Jude so my guard was down. The mother from the beach-chair family was already too close when she startled me by clearing her throat.

She was dragging along the older child, a girl with red hair, a reddened face, and red short-shorts—everything flecked with dark sand now—her eyebrows scrunched together in a tight knot. They both had tight knots between their eyebrows—two grimacing twins there to tell me something.

The mother spoke first.

"My daughter Bianca is very sensitive and she acts out when she can feel someone's energy too strongly."

She stared at me waiting for a reply, like this was the most normal conversation-starter in the world. Their four eyes were a steely green-gray, trying to pierce right through me.

"I'm just enjoying the ocean," I said, "It's my day off."

"Well, her force field extends about 50 yards in every direction."

"Force field?"

Bianca stood there, statue-still, but her mood had shifted. A feral smile tugged at her upper lip. I couldn't think of anything more mortifying than to be her right now, but she seemed to be starting to enjoy herself.

"You're wanting me to move farther away," I said, already knowing the answer so it wasn't really a question.

"Just down to the next rocky outcropping. It's not that far."

She pointed with a limp wrist like she was royalty, having come to our little Oregon beach town to regale us—her long, painted fingernail sharp at the tip. Bianca and I looked down the beach to see what she had in mind. "Otherwise our day will be ruined," she said. "Bianca can't help it—she just feels so much. She gets it from me."

I wanted to be outraged, but unfortunately I understood exactly what she meant, this keeping of distance. I knew this overwhelm of feeling but it had never occurred to me to demand space for myself. I nodded at them, pulled my jacket tighter around my chest and stood up.

"You should work on that," the mother said as an afterthought when I was already a couple steps away. "Your energy is very strong. Stronger—and to be frank—stranger than most. Bianca and I usually can't feel someone from so far away. It's...it's just too much. I'm not sure how you manage."

I had the fleeting thought they might be a family of aliens, here on Earth to experience base human emotions, to investigate everyone they met, running their tests and making mental notes. I took one more look at Bianca who was openly grinning now—she had unsettling straight, white teeth that looked to have been made in a factory. I decided not to respond to the mother. Bianca seemed to be fine standing near me even with all my supposed energy, but I didn't want to waste my time pointing that out. Without another word, I turned away from them to walk towards the new vantage point the mother had chosen for me. I could feel their eyes on my back, sharp little pinpricks.

The thing is, it wasn't the first time I had heard some version of this. One of my last lovers—not as hard to come by in a small town as one might think—told me I had pulled her like a magnet, like it was purely energetic and she didn't have a choice. She made it sound so non-consensual, which wasn't ideal.

"You're at your most attractive very close up," she said more than once, her lips vibrating against mine as she spoke, eyes wide open, seeing my every pore. "From farther away you can't see and feel this special thing you have."

We broke up after only a few months. While such a situation would have been ideal in my 20s, it felt unsustainable to be with someone who only found me appealing when a half-inch or less apart. So much of regular life is spent farther away and she wasn't interested in what she saw from any kind of distance. I'll admit the sex we had was hard to say goodbye to, but it wasn't enough to keep going.

The sand gave way under my shoes as I walked down the beach. The waves came up to greet me, coming so close and sneaking away, just like Jude. I didn't mind. I walked past the towering arched rock with its thick encrustation of barnacles exposed at low tide. I leaned over to listen to them chirping and squeaking—told them, as I always do, that they're my favorite musicians, though the morning birds on the bluffs and the frogs in the lake at dusk also have their appeal when the mood is right. The barnacles' song almost always lifts my mood—more than the birds and the frogs, who can sometimes sound so forlorn. The barnacles' high-pitched voices send the nerves at the base of my skull tingling and my whole body feels lighter. I've had the thought that when I retire, I'll have time to just sit next to them each day at low tide—if they're open to outsiders like me—and take the time to understand their language, to finally comprehend the gorgeous little messages they're sending.

When I got to the rock the mother had pointed me towards, I thought about sitting elsewhere just to spite her, but really, it was a perfect rock to sit on. I was surprised I'd never noticed it before—black with streaks of gray, thread-like veins and a curve that fit my butt as if it had been made for me. For some reason, I started thinking of that mean middle school boy who had said that thing about my face. It was such an odd thing to say, but rather creative, really, in hindsight. I couldn't remember his name. Conrad or Cody. I do remember he had a mullet and was the first boy in our grade to have his little mustache hairs sprout. It occurred to me that maybe someone had told him his face was bucket-like, and he was trying to pass it along. I imagined him now, middle aged—mustached, bearded, and still mulletted—and wondered if he was happy: if he liked his life and what he had done with his time here. Or if he was like me, kind of lonely when it came to other humans at least, and still looking for a way through.

I was about to turn 50 and had started experiencing a strange kind of dysphoria, not of gender—that was nothing new—but more of age. I remembered being a young child watching my grandmother put on her face powder, looking at herself in the gold-rimmed bathroom mirror. She was so alive, the most alive person I've ever known, and I always watched her closely. She was talking to me that day, but mostly talking to herself, explaining how disorienting it was to look in a mirror.

"I still feel like I'm twenty-five," she'd said. "I'm not totally sure how this happened." She patted her face gently and smiled down at me. She was in her 70s at the time. I wished she was still here so we could talk now that I understood all too well exactly what she'd meant.

When I looked in the mirror, I could see all my younger selves: they were right there, so close to the surface, but I wasn't sure at all what other people saw when they looked at me. Jude, for example. She is about ten years younger, without a wrinkle somehow, and her smooth face always glows a warm brown the minute the sun comes out. I wondered what she saw when she looked at me, which she did. Sometimes I caught her eyes lingering on me just a catch too long—at friends' dinner parties, at the post office, or at the grocery store—and my stomach fluttered ridiculously. But which version of me was she seeing?

More than seeing my younger selves, I wanted her to see what was underneath all that—the part of me that's hidden deep in the center of my body, layered over with bone and muscle and sinew and skin. In an Eastern Philosophy class I took in college, we learned about the koshas—that the innermost one is the hardest to access, tucked away underneath the veils of the body, the nervous system, and even consciousness. This is the part I wanted her to know, even as it often eluded me.

Maybe I should have just summoned my courage to ask what she felt in those lingering moments that made me dizzy with a disorienting ache. I didn't have anything to lose—maybe my dignity, which if I was being honest, has never been worth much.

An enormous seagull swooped overhead and landed on the wet sand nearby, pecking at a dead crab and eyeing me. He was beautiful with a robust, shimmering body and dark pink feet. He looked like he'd just been to the salon, so put together. Poor seagulls, they are relentlessly underappreciated creatures. He moved closer to me, stepped from side to side, and I understood he was trying to give me a message. I asked him if he came here often, told him he was a total babe. He already knew it. He ruffled his feathers and puffed up even bigger. A show off. I could have a crush on this bird, I thought.

Once I met a different seagull who I'm sure was Victor. Same eyes somehow. I asked him to tell me what had happened in that hotel room all those years ago. If it was an accident or not. When they found his body, it was twisted sickeningly with rigor mortis, face down on the yellow bathroom tiles. Accidental overdose of Fentanyl, the police report said. I didn't even know he had been into those kinds of drugs. I was under the impression when he died that he still shared everything with me and finding out he didn't was another layer of loss.

In the distance, I could see that the alien family had started packing up their chairs. Bianca looked cold now, rubbing her bare arms to warm herself. The father had not moved the whole time, just sat there looking like a grim baked-potato, but he was in motion now, dragging the chairs behind him up the embankment, leaving strange tracks in the sand. The little brother brought up the rear, covered in muck from head to toe. He stopped and turned around to look right back at me. He raised both middle fingers from his tiny fists to flip me off, maybe as a final test to see how I'd respond. I gave him a little salute before he turned to catch up.

The sky was getting heavier and the wind had picked up. Behind me was a thick expanse of wilderness that stretched for miles. No one ever goes in there; everyone just wants the beach. It's why they come here after all.

I closed my eyes for a moment, enjoying the sound of the waves crashing. I could smell a storm brewing.

As the wind picked up, I looked behind me again at the forest where I knew I would be more protected from the elements—I wasn't ready to go home yet. I walked towards that dark stand of trees that welcomed me easily. I picked my way along a narrow deer trail, jumped across a small creek, and crawled over two downed trees, rotting and covered with mushrooms. About a mile in, I was there: at the enormous rock that looks like a sea lion's head, where a hundred thousand years ago he flopped out of the sea and never left, decided to be stone instead. I read somewhere that sea lions are descendants of a bear-like terrestrial ancestor, so it makes sense he would be here, out of the salty depths and back to the trees where it all started.

I had been visiting this spot for years, drawn to it most strongly when melancholy threatened to overtake me. I always found solace there. That day was no different. I sat down and leaned against the sea lion bear and patted his shiny nose while the wet moss beneath me seeped into my jeans. No bother.

I laid all the way down, with the moss as a pillow, and started daydreaming about Jude. Not an unusual occurrence, but this one felt different, like maybe it could actually happen.

In my fantasy I imagined that just once a year, maybe in early September when the air here is the warmest, we would agree to meet in this place, hidden in the thick trees. We would have a pact not to tell anyone, regardless of if we were dating other people, and never to talk about it together before or after. We would meet there at sunset and probably not say anything. Maybe we would kiss—I hoped we would. Maybe we would smell that secret smell that lives low on the neck. Maybe we would take our clothes off and lay close against each other on a bed of redwood needles. We would be together in this different way to really try to see who we each were underneath all the skin and bone, to the innermost hidden kosha that needs so much protection.

I must have drifted into sleep because I woke up to a darkened sky, a bit of fading light coming through the trees. I brushed myself off, gave the sea lion bear a pat and headed out, taking deep breaths and rubbing the sleep out of my eyes.

When I made it back to the beach, the sun was setting behind thick clouds on the horizon and the sky was saturated with burnt orange. I started making my way back towards the river trail that would take me home.

In the distance ahead of me, was a lone figure—a silhouetted body I had memorized a thousand times, rabbit-smooth and vital. She waved and called my name—started walking directly to where I stood.

I waited there for her with the trees at my back and the ocean before me—humming with all my energy—alive, alive, alive.

we talked about you in class today – Mailene (she/they)

CW: Sexual Assault

you and my professor have something in common
you both said that i shouldn't have gone over dressed like that
my chest too exposed
my jeans too ripped
i was practically begging for it

we were just supposed to watch a movie
i told you before, i didn't want to do anything else

16 and 23
sixteen. twenty-three.

i guess it's true, men's brains develop later than women's, *because* the word consent rang no bells for you.

so you continued to get closer and closer
despite the fact that i was screaming no
...wait, was i?
maybe i just wasn't loud enough

and so you continued to pin me down
despite the fact that i shoved you off me
—you thought i was joking

120 pounds and 250 pounds
one hundred twenty. two hundred and fifty.

you told me to stop "squirming so much"
unarmed. armed.
gun.
gun.
gun.

how was i supposed to leave when there was a gun?

how does one fight back at gunpoint?

at that moment, i chose to surrender
at that moment, i chose life

i threw away everything i wore that day.

my favorite shirt
brand new jeans
my comfiest shoes

i scrubbed every inch of my body until i bled.

i brushed my teeth until my arm gave out
the funny part was, until today i thought i had moved on from you. you know, healed.

i realized it was just a quick fix.
a band aid over a bullet hole.

but my teacher, like one of my closest friends at the time, had to remind me:
i asked for it
because who was i to think a grown man could simply hang out with me without needing to most literally rip off my clothes

after i left class, i scrubbed until i bled again
brushed my teeth until my arm gave out
couldn't sleep with the lights off
because now, every time i close my eyes

i'm taken back to you.
and those soulless eyes.
hovering over me while i beg you.

to
just
let
me
leave.

let. me. leave.

we talked about you in class today.

Moon Sister – László Aranyi (he/her)

Awakening – László Aranyi (he/her)

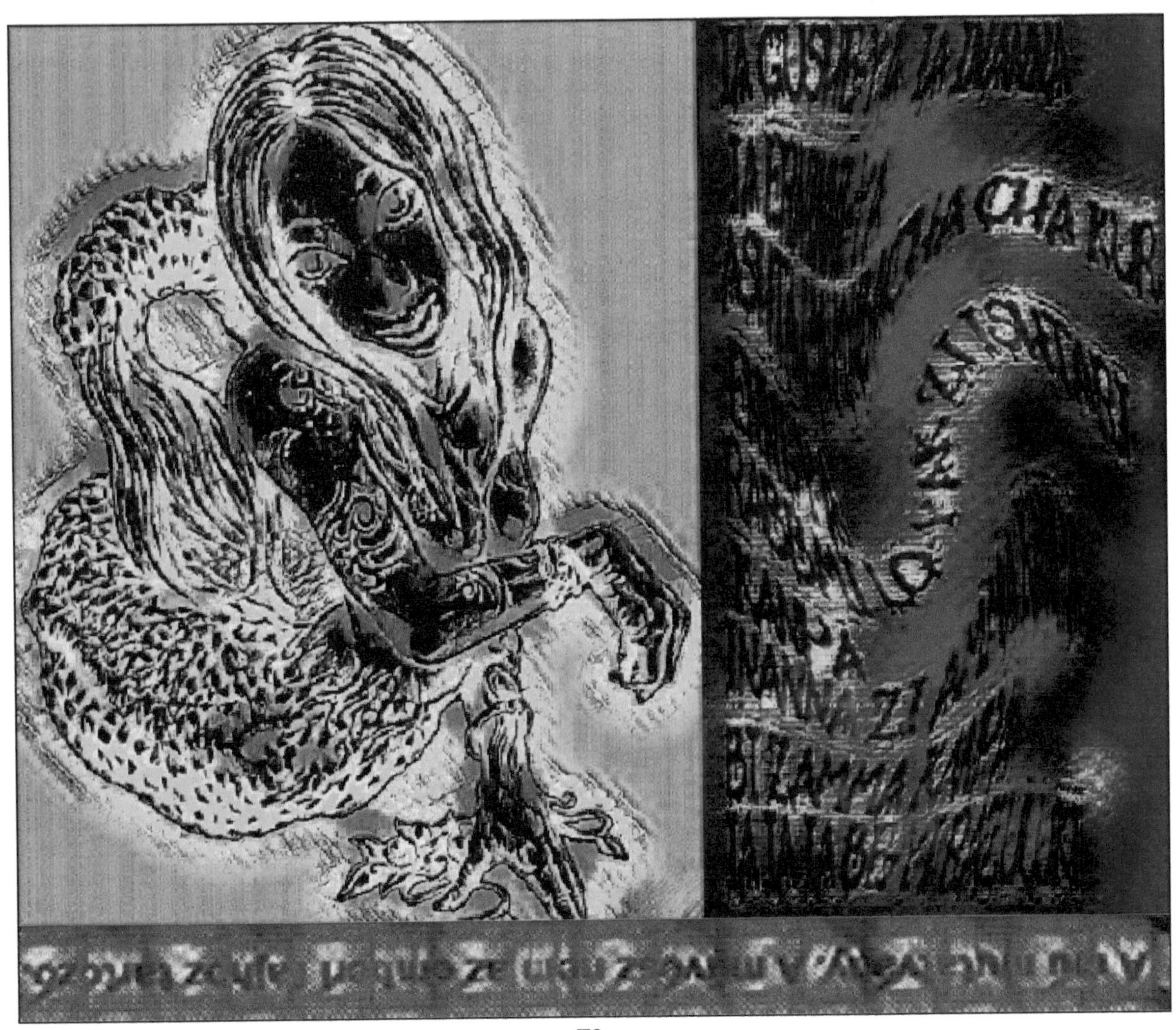

Set me Free – Syd M. (they/them)

Months of being unable to recognize myself,
In the reflection of the dresser,
with Raven hair that extends past my shoulders,
Blackened bags under the lashes,
Balls of skin that shake and annoy,
I look feminine now;

أنا أكره ذلك.[1]
هذا الجسد ليس جسدي.[2]

Mama said that I look better this way,
Away from nonconformity,
Wear dresses, perfume, makeup, jewelry,
She said, *You're a pretty girl, what's in your head, doesn't matter;*

انا لست انت[3]
هذا الجسم ليس لك[4]

After working hard to earn the means,
To experience liberty and independence,
For myself and myself alone,
I went to my hair stylist,
You won't look feminine anymore,
Think about what you are choosing,
Why are you here today?

جسدي اختياري[5]
حررني[6]

Scissors begin to trim the raven,
Weights lift off my chest,
As the bits of hair rain down past my arms,
I see them, I see my reflection for the first time in months,
A spontaneous smile erupts,
Mama and Baba's little girl is gone, good riddance;

هذا الجسد لي[7]

حُرّيتي أن أكون كما لا يريدون لي أن أكون[8]

Arabic Translations—
1: I hate it
2: My body is not mine
3:I am not you
4: This body is not yours
5: My body, my choice
6: Liberate me
7: This body is mine
8: My freedom is to be what they don't want me to be

when i cum – Joseph Soares (he/him)

when i cum i do it
as an act of self-immolation
an act of defiance and protest
don't confuse me for a hedonist
though i admit that pleasure
is a halo of hope and dear god
my moaning is a brittle prayer
whispered through stained glass
these acts of impulse the only way
to tame our passions

greeting cards make me dysphoric – Joseph Soares (he/him)

my self-image was nearly pristine
until running into Gender Trouble
at Shoppers Drug Mart.
my gender is a grease-trap
with a deep fetish
for the immaterial;
it needs to be cleaned out
before closing time.

elder – Joseph Soares (he/him)

When I say I feel old, don't try to dissuade me. Because if you do, you don't know what I mean. What I mean is that the life expectancy of someone like me is thirty-two at best, or twenty-five at worst. I just turned twenty-five. What I mean is that I'm supposed to get my blood pressure checked once a week. What I mean is that, often, I feel like I'm at the end of my rope, the one hanging in the garage in 2014. What I mean is that I had to get an ECG done because I was having heart palpitations. What I mean is that my memory is starting to go, and my lungs feel like they're caked with butter. What I mean is that there's blood in my urine and I don't know what that's about. What I mean is that it feels like I have a longer medication list than I have a list of accomplishments and I don't know if that'll ever change. What I mean is that my cousin had breast cancer at twenty-three and my aunt had a heart-attack at thirty-five. What I mean is that people like me don't last very long in these parts anyway.

concrete christening – Joseph Soares (he/him)

Where would we be
If not for softened prayers,
Hands clasped tight
Thinking not now,
Not this.

(Ceremonial kneeling on fresh pavement
The closest we get to wholesale forgiveness)

Where would we be
If not for the lost time
Those years that haunt us
That we should embrace
Because at least now we know
How to lose ourselves.

Blood – Zo Copeland (they/them)

Just to rub it in
All the times they she me
All the times they her me
And never heard me

Just to twist the knife
With your 'is that Miss or Mrs?'
With your 'how can I help you madam?'
Your polite conversational bullets

Just to punch harder
Through the tick box of male or female
Through the 'error: field required'
I have failed the test of the system
(or has the system failed me?)

Just to deepen the dig
Of the Mens room
Of the Ladies room
The no In-Between or Neither-Nor room

Just to slam me when I'm down
By questioning who I am
By questioning what's in my pants
The answer is: blood.

Coming Out Spoons – Zo Copeland (they/them)

Naively thinking
Coming out
Would be a one-time thing
(but it became an endless repetition of a thing)

Naively thinking
Coming out
Would be a sexual orientation thing
(but it also became a gender thing)

Naively thinking
Coming out
Would be a statement sort of thing
(but it became a barrage of opinions and questions thing)

And each time it required spoons
One spoon to interject them 'he-ing' my partner
Another spoon to breathe through their surprise
(and yet another to swallow their over-apology)

One spoon to consider if it was safe
Another spoon to assert my gayness
Yet another to wait for some kind of response
(their sister, their neighbour, someone from school)

Two spoons to assess their gender politics
Another spoon to decide whether I have enough spoons
Yet another two to work out the language and tell them
(and then to explain it)

Two spoons to find the courage and harness it
Another two to introduce myself with pronouns
Yet another to deal with the stares
(for the rest of the meeting)

One spoon to consider how they'll respond to my clothes
Another to assess safety in holding your hand
Yet another two to ignore harassment
(the last of my spoons)

Necessary damage
To my armoury of spoons
Such a futile weapon
With which to enter battle

dacryphile (bitch) – Andrew Michael Joseph (he/him)
44" x 36" silver leaf on wheat-pasted pigment print, 2022

no shade in the shadow of the cross – Andrew Michael Joseph (he/him)
24" x 16" archival pigment print, 2022

the kiss – Andrew Michael Joseph (he/him)
24" x 16" archival pigment print, 2022

coalesce – Andrew Michael Joseph (he/him)
36" x 24" archival pigment print, 2022

barren eve – Andrew Michael Joseph (he/him)

36" x 24" archival pigment print, 2023

Pérez Women Have Always Been Beautiful – Bianca Alyssa Pérez (she/her/hers/ella)

in their act of taking apart something to make
a new thing. A shedding my skin feasts on.

I see my face in the tearing of a soft
tortilla. It's all about amor[1] here—roll the tortilla up

con amor[2], drown the tortilla in oil *con amor*
flip it over *con amor*.
Today, my flautas do not burn. Today,
I'm reminded that I'm

my grandmother's flesh. Hot oil
pops onto my thumb
and I don't wince. This is the way to loving my body —

to breathing the burns on my fingers, my wrists, my palms.
Each burn, a time I cooked a meal for myself.

Sat down at the dinner table with myself. Passed the salt to myself.
Blessed my food the same way my grandmother did.

---

[1] Love
[2] With love

Waiting for the Rumble of a Border Crashing Down – Bianca Alyssa Pérez (she/her/hers/ella)
—after Audre Lorde

I am a woman past midnight,
walking home, whispering
to the fear on my back
that I won't die tonight,
not tonight. It doesn't want to listen.

I am a pink lipgloss woman
who, in a fit of anger
and shame, will wipe my lips
harshly on a bar napkin
because a man stared
too hard, asking what dirty words
I can moan in Spanish.

I am a woman begging
not to be devoured—
a generation of women waiting
for the silence of a blunt edge.

I am tired
of the weight of Fear
clawing its name onto my back.

I am a fetish of a woman,
a breathing feast,
a grieving cat-call,
angry about my keychain knife
and fast-walking legs.

I Came from a Ribcage, First – Bianca Alyssa Pérez (she/her/hers/ella)

from the gorged belly
of a tree, half rot, half million-ringed
life under bark, I screamed myself alive.
Before this, I died made of gunpowder
singed against the flesh of my left leg's calf.
This is to say, this body my body sweet body
must be torch-fired into hot skillet pain or amber
fireworks blazed behind my eyelids.
I am made of saltwater
crystallized into a pillar of woman.
Somedays, I am afraid I am made of my father,
tobacco-ground and stuffed between clenched teeth.
An ant-pile of the things I do not say festers quietly
in a Gemini sun, warm flakes of secrets carried on my back:
the cigarette I smoked at 17 with a boy in the backseat of his mom's car,
the first time I touched myself because I needed to feel
something other than alone,
I do not eat enough, I recite the alphabet to fall asleep,
I recite the alphabet while twisting an apple stalk.
And in the space between
my pelvis and kidney,
a mountain breaks open,
oozing an ache that buries me.
And from a ribcage, there I was.
Descendent of calcified sin.

What I Will Not Tell My Grandmother – Bianca Alyssa Pérez (she/her/hers/ella)

Despite my mispronounced devotion
and the echo of something extranjera[3] in the cave
of my throat, I speak to the saints in Spanish.
They understand me perfectly.

.

In my mouth, locusts hum a gospel.
Swarming in the dark,
they roll my estranged tongue onto itself.
I let them.

My tongue, finally, wraps around my neck.
A bleeding muscle slithering, tempting silence.
Soon, I will become the prayed-to saint,
holding la luna[4] below the Virgin Maria's bare feet

.

Candles, like secrets crackling in my ears, burn quietly.
As the wick turns black, I recite the prayers in whispered confession.
The saints will listen if I speak the language
that my grandmother taught me over the comal[5].

In sainthood, I revel.
The sheep follow me through fields of burning bushes
and their blind faith scorches along with everything else.
The stench of my unraveling trails in a horde behind us.

I am closer to a heaven
I cannot name.
One day it will arrive on its knees,
with my grandmother's voice in palm,
sounding like all the times
she blessed me out the door.

---

[3] foreign
[4] The moon
[5] griddle

I Am My Own Haunting – Bianca Alyssa Pérez (she/her/hers/ella)

my hands a ghost brushing
my hair in the mirror
in the mirror is a woman
that i do not recognize
her mouth unhinges
a thousand crickets swarm
from her tongue my tongue
a phantom muscle that has forgotten
how to twist into itself i spit and my dead father's name
spills out oozes out withering i am a haunted house
of prayers to the walls revelations distorted into whispers
a kitchen is a hallway is a door is a
basement is a bedroom is a sleeping woman
witnessing my own face convulse i am a nightmare
the exorcism of a body that does not belong to me i am
breathing into her lungs gasping for air
ghost touch waiting for skin
my name coming up
from beneath the floorboards
like cigarette smoke

bless-id be thy kingdom – j.g. bova (he/they)

wherein lie the liars of the crypt
robbers of the tomb of jesus
christ be damned to thy name
shouting idiocies in solemn Salem by drive-by crusade

wherein the devils roam to rebel against hell-themed playplaces
demons defined by defiance to
words whose ink bleed into lost
Souls searching for purpose

wherein angels believe that teachings of the prophet
portend only to the few that remain
on top of the white throne of bones from those they ripped apart
with bless-id biblical beliefs
cross of sacrifice hung on the rear-view mirror

wherein these enlightened few can
take the no grace to plaster in the face of the queer devils that roam
outside of hell's boundary
for certainty of completing such righteous acts in the name of
their version of god—one that surely
carries the acceptance of all people
except those who are not of
creamy complexion and straight trajectory with such
yearning for violence against those which oppose their rigid systems
built upon the lies of categories like rows of suburban streets

wherein lie of liars masculine tyranny

wherein men lose hearts
in pursuit of religious entitlement

but the hell you believe is empty and the devils are here to stay

to navigate an uncharted bit of marsh – j.g. bova (he/they)

careful now
pull up boots as far as can be after leaving the comfort of reshaped trees
careful step as mud sloshes beneath footprints that smashed giant toads

look there
avoid areas where the marsh wiggles with glee in hopes of bringing you back to nature
to make you one with the seas yet again
mark your map with the steps of forgotten bits of this island melting down into ocean

look back
as footsteps wash away but the marsh's
stomach growls to beckon you deeper

careful now(here)

rip your boots from your feet
feel the slimy land engulf your toes
listen to the earth call you back home

look now
as fresh marks tremble to restful oblivion
mud sloshes beneath and around
quill ink spills black into watery depths
like squids that spectate such spectacles of true exploration

careful (nowhere)
feel in steps yet to come

i beg of you
follow me
through uncharted sea

beyond civilization – j.g. bova (he/they)

sing to me of festival, nay please shout
lure forth with lilac: Aphrodite's sprout

find solace between blues and pinks
of sunset, lavender haze
creep up on time before it
does so to you

performance: an act of nowness
do not let yourself dwell only on stage
from age to thus we face such wars

sparkle there in endless time
twirling vines in a dress
by cliff, by creek, dance cheek-to-cheek
answer no questions

your colors, your vibrant soul
wake each morning beside seas
pushing, pulling with gravity

the sky the moon are but old friends
set sights on cosmos
beyond the bend

and be not bound by petty binary
for it's their knowledge that needs refinery

you don't have to be sorry
greet the stars on the way beyond
for the empty universe is a
blank stale for you—sweet child

romanticizing the finality of it all – j.g. bova (he/they)

is it cliché to say that this is a cold embrace? that this is a door closing? what if this moment is just one of many to befall me? what if i am to come along again as a dove, an antelope, a dragon, a chair, a space between atoms, or even dark nothingness? what if the next step in existence is but another step? what if this coda is but the beginning of a crossfade into another hymn? what happens if i leave behind my field unplowed as the sweet summer dew glistens? what happens if i leave my spaceship on autopilot as i fade into a star's warm embrace? what happens if i linger in a blackhole only to get pushed out into another universe as a fragment-like flea on a spaghetti-like swirling space worm? what if i close my eyes one night to find that i am but a fish with legs pulling on the banks of river and gasping this first breath of raw air? and is it cliché to think that there is another existence—is it selfish to think myself worthy of such another chance to channel my being into another body of sorts? well, what happens now? does anyone hear my pleas as i fall into this cavern? this sea? this bed? this book? this one last stop? does a steam train keep moving when the coal ceases to exist and tracks follow in line? when will questions cease?

everything still

obit for youth: 2000 – 2021 – j.g. bova (he/they)

born on the moment of millennium they were finding their way through suburbs as ravens encircled their sorrowfilled soul - they never really got to feel grass between their toes or sand through their fingers or water washing over their spongey brain or the freedom of wearing a dress

their body lays on the church parking lot where they were found at dawn

died on the eve of new year, youth leaves behind familial connection - a mutual understanding that their next life wouldn't be in the way parents might have thought; a mutual understanding that their reincarnation would go down a path with wild colors - bricks painted with yellow, white of snow shimmering, lavender skies, and deep black space ahead

their skin so soft, almost as if they had used skincare products - confusing - their eyes clasped upon the stars in the galaxy, though glazed over ever so slightly - ringing in time with angry phones calls because they missed their curfew

their body moves just as they were found at dawn.

Woman at Sea – S. Kavi (she/her)

Catch Sight 1 – Anna Laura Falvey (she/her)

A preface: this is all in my brain
and doesn't make it all the way down
to my heart. These are things that I see,
little noticings. You know, around. Little

baby noticings. I'll start with the obvious:

kitchen plates. There is the matching set,
plastic and sturdy with inevitable rooster
farm medallion motifs printed on each:
one bluer, one more gold. Both with little red
jabs in flower and eye, long raised scratches

where we've sawed through tough pieces of
goodthickbread, some arresting orange blots
of calabrian chili oil that haven't scrubbed out.
These are invariably breakfast plates, always
in use; the first to clatter to the tile floor

when the dishrack is overfull. Next,

on the doorframe, a sweet breath of blue
paint prints where your fingers rested

when leaving the room after you painted.
This is usually where I can see your ghost

most clearly, actually. When I'm sat
on the couch (we're two couches past

on the timeline) with my knees drawn
tight to my chest, looking at the door.
Behind my immediate vision is a smoked
out still of you standing with your hand,

clouded and tacky with layers of blue
acrylic, resting on the doorframe.

We look at each other, but if I'm honest,
I don't think you see me.

You couldn't. The next is obvious:

it’s the faint pencil marks
15 inches or so above the bed
near the foot that I can’t erase
and never bothered to buy white

paint to efface the traces of.
We tried to hang a shelf
on the wall; the lines you sketched
out with dumb, apparently magic

permanent pencil are perfectly level.
The room, we began to discover,
and I would confirm after you left,
is a brick box. Brick hard like toothbone,

but impossible to drill into. I covered
the shallow dusted cavities I made
trying to find the soft, the tissue part
of the wall with postcards and photos,

a botanical poster of pomegranate
plants, a poem I heard. The faint
pencil marks connect these parts
like veins under thin paper skin.

Catch Sight 2 – Anna Laura Falvey (she/her)

Ella has filled your old tiny studio
with a comically large peace lily
and a potato she let sprout and
climb across the walls
and an absolutely thriving
avocado plant that she grew
from pit, and revived
an old plant of yours
that I almost let die.
The patter of blue paint
that marks the floor is covered
with her bed, pushed into the corner
to make space for more life; with
her rubber soled, pink
felted slippers. The room
is filled with oxygen. Laughter
and laughter cycled up and through
the green, breathe
in, and out.

Sarah has your toolkit. It's big
and sturdy canvas, and I saw it
all packed before she toted it off
to her new studio in Sunset Park.
She is an impressive and persistent
packer. It was so full, it wasn't closed.
An open-mouthed cube, hand drill
draped across the top as though
it were a chaise. She took your toolkit,
your hunched silver desklamp
(paintstained), and your orange chair
and now they are all new. She makes little
things and big things, little worlds
and worlds bigger.

Thai uses your cookware
better, god, better than you
ever could. I like sitting
at the kitchen table talking
with her while she cooks.

Sometimes, if we're having
a conversation that distracts
her enough, she cooks intuitively,
not paying attention at all to
what she's doing, her hands
moving softly on their own
while her mind is elsewhere:
onions to chop, the slow
chhhhhnk of the knife slicing
through to the cutting board.
She shakes mushroom powder
into the ancientmagic simmer
of the pot. and again. and again.
and again. absently; I'm not certain
she realizes it. When she's done,
she tastes the soup, nods,
and says, *umami*. She ladles
me a bowlful, and she is beautiful
and she is warm, and I am beautiful
and I am warm again.

miranda, facedown in the sand at lands end – Anna Laura Falvey (she/her)

girl washes ashore in sf on saturday
evening (around 8pm, night *young* young),
dress limp, wet, hanging, and pushes
her chest off the ground, spits (not dainty. no
manners. exile island girl). she slings her feet
through the slickness of the shore sands
up the beach to the dim orange streetlamps above,
towards the slit of moon hanging still in indigo.

a pair of white pupils glints into view,
beasting noise though the pitch. behind
these eyes, '62 pontiac tempest (ha)
crunches to a halt, drivers'side window
at her eyelevel. the window cranks down,
squeaking dully with mist, and a broad gold
arm perches heavily on the sill.
"hey,"
calls a voice, the sound of a wave in her ear,
rough and whole as matter, transient as shore
she wants to touch it.
"you need a ride?"
their face appears in the empty window frame:
slender and strong, a graceful tilt to the eyebrow,
What is't? A spirit? she thinks
their hair mooncolored with a rosy tinge, stuck
up at all angles, a compass confused.
she wants to touch it.
lips: laughing, smooth, teeth bared a grin
"where ya headed?"
eyes: a slowmoving greygreen, saltchuck.
she drowns. slips into the passenger seat

and out onto the light-pricked street they drive.
It carries a brave form. But 'tis a spirit. she assures
herself. In the dim, vibrating safety of the car,
they lift a finger, hands deftly calloused
(shewantstotouchthem) to the radio, flicking
through the airwaves to settle on joplin raking
her vocal cords like a leaf-covered street.

they course through the city like blood
through a vein while the sky inks to
darker night. the driver speaks in spirit
history, pointing out memory: a lover's strut ghosted
up one block; a dog-walking gig yanked down another;
a strip of greenish where they dropped
a hammered silver mountain necklace
(devastating, a gift from their mother, worn everyday);
a bar nestled on a streetcorner where they had
gotten toodrunk at a beat-poetry reading;
two corners down where they'd lost
these same drinks, their pals' (fellow spirits)
heads thrown back in shrieking laughter. they ask
if her story bore any of this city's marrow.
'Tis far off,
she replies,
And rather like a dream than an assurance
That my remembrance warrants.

the shades of night click into place,
and the tempest rolls into park beneath
a flickering white lamp. together the two
walk slowly down the street and up another
until they reach a warmly burning neon sign:
wild side west "it's pretty new,
but pretty far out. hang on a sec—"
they slip their fingers into the shallow
pocket of their brown corduroy coat
and pull out a packet of cigarettes, jaw cutting
fog as they perch it, a bird between their lips.
she watches the ember glow to life eyes
shifting orange inhale hold exhale
a stormcloud, dissolving into the thick grey air.
she wants to be part of their inhale, to be held
in the cave of their mouth and tenderly released
between their lips. she wants to touch it. (*Hence,*
bashful cunning And prompt me,
plain and holy innocence)

she does.
on their next breath out, she pulls her fingers slow slow
through their drag, disrupting the smoke to swirl.
I would not wish Any companion in the world
but you Nor can imagination form a shape,

besides yourself, to like of, she says in one breath.
their mouth parts surprise, cigarette balanced
on their lower lip and grin
a wide and beaming wicked joy wicked joy.

If the ill spirit have so fair a house,
Good things will strive to dwell within't,
she thinks as they wrap their arm
around her waist as firmly and gracefully
as a vine grows round a seawreck, holding
the shards of wood in place. together

the two push open the door into the dim
and twinkling blast of warm air—an island
peopled with magic and shimmering heat.
Spirits, she realizes, gaze ebbing in tidal
pull across the room: spirits moving joy
across the darkwood floor on trays, setting
glasses of amber fizz down in front of still
more spirits, spirits with hair long and tousling,
lips full and rosy, dresses that cling to hips
and sway like kelp: flow in contrast to the twang
of music playing; spirits in soft dark-buttoned
shirts, short buzztop hair tucked; spirits embracing,
beautiful bodies melted together; spirits flickering
angled spirits inclined spirits desire overwhelmed
her eyes, glass (*I am a fool To weep at what I am glad of*)
a spirit appeared before her like the quick snap
of a bonfire log, wild grin to match wilder hair,
mass of curls piled high on the head tied back
in a cheetah-print ribbon. *hiya, fern*—she addresses
the driver—*back table's free, head over*
and i'll get you and your friend a beer,
o.k.? a hand lingers on her shoulder
before ribbon spirit disappears, a hand that says
i see you you're here i see you you're here.

O, wonder!

fern leads miranda by hand through the spiritland.
her eyes fill with tears, the bar's gold light refracted
she thinks:
O brave new world That has such people in't!

How to perceive myself as desirable?, An Architecture – Anna Laura Falvey (she/her)

I was in the bathtub on Sunday
afternoon with someone I love
and they had their arms around me

and god I just felt so cozy. I have to
say: I don't know how to write about
myself beautifully. I always want

to describe my body as something
architectural, something geologic,
no life, no heat, a cool cobblestone

street to look up and down, a piece
of roughtouch rock with some kind
of interesting texture: unknowable,

there. In the bathtub, I don't feel like
a rock. I do feel soft. my shoulders
kissed over by the milky water,

my cheek pressed to their chest,
their hand on my back. Here, usually,
I am tempted to take the image apart.

It's when it's soft and comfortable
and lovely that I start wanting to
describe them wetting their hands like

a tragic potter molding my clay shoulders
into thick wings folded back in rest;
or

I become epsom salt flowering powder
through their fingers and I am nothing
but the torn skin of my cuticles

screaming in salt salt burning
and I dissolve by the warm
water's ruly mercy and I release

the tension in their thighs,
in their forearms, in their beautiful hands,
I am healing and I am gone. They breathe

me in and I am gone. I am

gone. See?

This is where my mind goes.

My shoulders.
Are.
Soft.
Silky?
No, milky. Kissed over
by the milky water. Kissed
over by
over by

I am afraid, sometimes.

i started using a menstrual cup and this cycle has been different – Emily Perkovich (she/her)

**CW – visual images of blood, mentions of menstruation & sexual abuse*

The first time I used a tampon I broke my hymen

The first time I had sex didn't hurt

Well, it hurt, but not inside

Well inside, but not my cervix

The cervix is the window to the heart

Or something

I'm saying that I said no, but we were young, and it was our first time, and I didn't know yet that no could mean no

We don't fuck anymore, but we're still friends, and once he told the room at large about how he likes to "skull-fuck his wife's mouth upside down"

Is she smiling or is that a frown?

Smile once for yes and frown upside down for no

The disgust I feel with my blood left some time in my teens, but body and blood aren't the same thing, just ask the savior

/not my savior, but you know the guy, the martyr, the one who knows a guy, the here, hold my beer guy that can do it all with no fear guy, the jack of all trades guy, the guy who plays guitar, totally respects women, but what's a g-spot? And what's the clit? And I like to skull-fuck my wife, but I'm a hopeless romantic, and would totally die for you, guy/

The disgust I feel for my body ebbs and flows and it's easiest to see low vs high tide by checking my hemline

There's something about a clump of tissue-soaked rags that screams dissociate

There's something about the way the crimson hits the basin, puddles across the surface-tension, spills and clots like watercolors that screams immersion

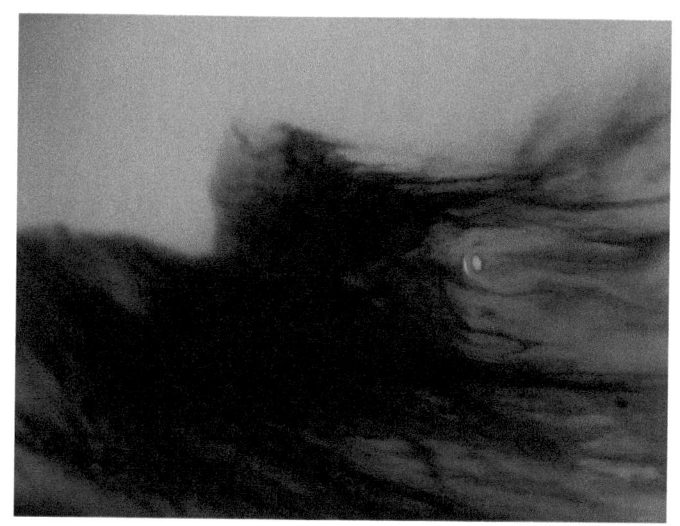

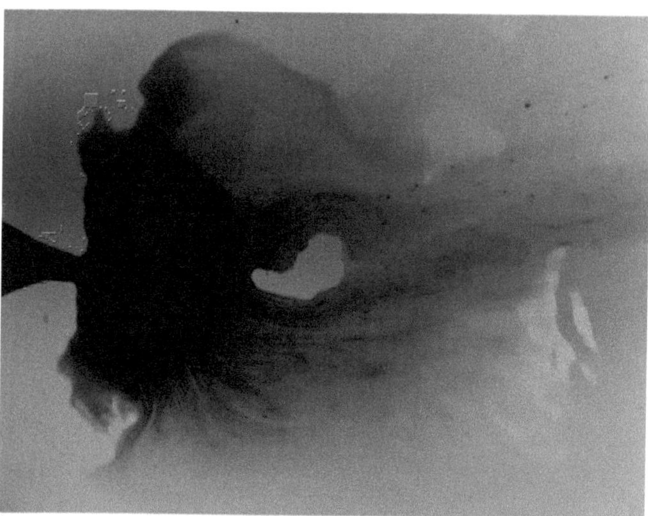

On Being 25 – Francesca Kritikos (she/her)

I'm the same weight my mother was
on her wedding day

She was my age
and wore a dress I'd never wear

I'm an inch taller than her
with a wider jaw
and broader shoulders

As for my men
they've been fewer
but worse

What I'm trying to say is
do you want to know me

Sunrise Countdown – Francesca Kritikos (she/her)

In the morning
I wake to men

Kicking bottles, throttling
cars that won't start

Shoving garbage
into garbage

Sunrise countdown
to collateral damage

In the morning
I wait in bed

for the crack of glass
on the back of my head

Mountains Make a Victim of the Earth – Francesca Kritikos (she/her)

I've seen how

You can stand up a little taller
with my body under yours

The plates of my hips
razed

Your fingers shoved in the gap
of my clavicle

Don't worry
no one else can see

You're lucky
I'm not used to being free

A Pregnant Woman and The Child Who Built a Home Out of His Father's Rage – Anushka (she/her)

OPENING ACT

A child lays in the embrace of a tree in the middle of a barren land. The child wears a sad face as if he's already tired of nature's torments, but his eyes are still closed. How has he even seen enough of the world to have grief hit him in the bones?

The tree makes an offering of a poisonous apple to the sleeping child.

A woman with a huge pregnant belly works in the field. A child cries in the distance. She doesn't recognize it, but her husband is calling her name. She freezes. He's called her name for the third time.

THE CRIME

The husband is sitting on the bed with his shirt on the floor and his feet placed over it.

The woman enters.

Woman: Did you call?
Husband: 'Course I did. What do you think you have been doing there?
Woman: I have been working in the fields. Our crops are nearly dying.
Husband: You are such a bitch. I called you 10 times and you didn't even hear me. There isn't any need for you to work in the field. I am the man of this house. It's my work. You have only one responsibility and that is to take care of the house.

The husband comes closer to the pregnant wife and grabs her by her hair. The wife winces.

The husband begins to speak in a low, muffled voice only the wife can hear.

Husband: You know what? You deserve to be here inside the house. Don't try to steal my job. What were you trying to do, huh?

A thought passes through the husband's mind as he smiles and speaks.

Husband: Did you find some man out in the field who loves your impure body? This is why you go there, huh?

He pulls her by the hair twice more. She almost screams but instead whimpers.

Husband: Shush. Don't you dare. Trying to show the village how cruel your husband is? How he makes you work even when you are pregnant? Bitch. I wish I could kill you and this child, right now.

The husband drags the wife to the bed and lays her down. He locks the door from the inside to destroy any potential of witnesses to his crime.

THE AFTERMATH

It's been hours since the villagers heard the woman cry. For this occasion, all of them wore the right expression of measured curiosity mixed with undertones of sorrow.

Humans are the only animals who can be calculative in the face of despair.

The woman weeps with her back against the wall. Her eyes are bloodshot and the space between her legs is crimson red.

The child, who was laying in the embrace of the tree, wakes up. The tree tells the child in its raucous voice that the time to go is crawling closer. But then.

IT'S TIME TO GO

The wife howls and beats her stomach 'til there's only blood on the floor. She can't give up the child, it'll make her a bad wife and a bad mother. She can't have the child when its footprints match the ones of its father. She can't have the child 'cause giving it this life will already make her the worst mother. A mother who couldn't even save her own flesh from the hands of fate. She weeps and weeps. But it's too late.

The screams grow louder and the crowd around the cottage grows in size and power. The people look at each other as if to weigh the sorrow of a mother and the blooming of one's life out of the blood-soaked land. Who wins? Who holds more importance?

The tree speaks to the sleeping child, lowering its eyes in shame.

Tree: There is no other way to go, son. It's time to go

THE CLOSING ACT

Believe the mother, she tried her best to save you, but the world failed you two.

Eleven years later, the voice echoes in the child's ears and every word seems to spell out the truth for him.

The mother is gone. Dead.

After 4 years of an impending doom looming over the fragile figure, the day arrived and the curse of a woman's sorrow took her away into the arms of the same tree that once held the boy.

The boy tried to make a home out of the walls his father shattered in rage. He tried his best to live happily ever after, but what's one to do when the devil you feared your whole life is the devil who always hides inside your own home?

You Know It, You Saw It – Anushka (she/her)

Somewhere in the dark
There are sirens going off
About a crime that was never committed.

You know it,
You saw it.

You press your hands together
And hold them tightly against your chest
Hoping against all the possibilities in the world
That the sun arrives not before noon tomorrow.

You are standing in the middle of the road
At 3 in the morning
While you hear the reckless sound
Of the blurred sirens from afar.

You rewind the scenes one by one
Holding them delicately against the frame of your brain,
As you allow them to flood your memory one by one.

The chainsaw resting admirably
On the centre table of the room
That was only ever built for expensive crockery,
Something peculiar about the scene stings you in the palm.

You know it,
You saw it.

The windows are all wide open,
The wind crawls in with a rush
As if it was being chased by the sirens
Of a crime about to be committed.

You let your feet drag you to another room
Where you didn't have to look around
To know where you were,
You just knew through its fragrance.

You open the first drawer
Only to find a wounded sparrow lying there
Layered in bandages,
It looks at you with broken glass eyes.

You know it,
You saw it.

You move back to the room
Where the chainsaw once rested,
But was now gone,
Escaped into the thin air.

You look through the window
And you find the chainsaw flying
Into the torpefied wind of the midnight.

You know it,
You saw it.

But the chainsaw strikes you
And now you have no eyes,
No witnesses to prove anything that happens next,
Or to prove what happened before.

You knew it,
And you did see it.

You saw the chainsaw lying admirably,
But you also saw the body of a man lying.
Something peculiar that stung your palm
Was the blood on the tips of the guitar
Placed behind the head of the man.

You know it
'cause you saw it.

When you saw the sparrow lying in the first drawer,
It was a lie
'cause you saw a lifeless woman's hand.

You opened all the other drawers
And found her body stuffed their like a
Disgraceful baggage of a stubborn father.

You know it
'cause you saw it.

The windows weren't open,
You pushed them wide open.
You dialled 911 and called the police,
You wanted the woman in the drawer caught.

You threw the chainsaw out of the window,
But before that,
You used it on your eyes
So that they fell out of their sockets.

You know it,
You saw it,
And you did it.

"No eye witnesses were found on ground, sir."
"I think the woman did it."
"She killed him with the guitar
And then hid pieces of herself in the drawers."

You left the house like the wind that once rushed in,
Haunted by the sirens in the middle of the night
You found your way, far away, on the deserted ground.

You still have her rubies to trade,
The ones you found on her neck.
You still have parts of her body to sell.

You know it,
You saw it
And you did it.

A blind man did the killing and the innocent wife and husband had to pay the price of their lives.
—a newspaper headline.

'Til My Soul Snaps – Anushka (she/her)

Hurried steps/ broken cobblestones/ tainted sidewalks/ blurred spray paints/ empty stomach/ a veiled face/ long sleeves/ brother's tattered shirt/ mom's inner/ father's shredded trousers/ hands on clothes/ trying to pull them long/ eyes search for another figure/ but there's no one/ shallow breaths/ followed by one long sigh/ pulls at the sleeves/ stumble on her steps/ eyes keeping check of another figure in the dark/ "what was the crime?"/ the whispers say in the dark/ "why are you so afraid?"/ they say in broad daylight/ police, prisons or the law?/ they make assumptions/ I bite the words/ for I know they will bleed acid on their suspicions/ I am afraid of death/ and/ my crime is that I'm a woman.

Eyes on the floor/ your head's spinning/ as the words pierce through your chest/ there's dirt under your father's feet/ but he's too concerned with the dress you are wearing/ it exposes your thighs, just a little part of your torso, and your arms a little too much/ you're a rebel/ they say/ you're lucky/ they whisper/ because you can go against his wishes/ but they don't know he thinks you're just a slut/ the kind of woman who isn't dignified enough/ to cover herself up/ he says/ "Look at your mom."/ but what do you look at her for?/ the sorrow she hides?/ the fact that she knows the kind of women you sleep with?/ what do you learn from her?/ how to never love a man like her husband?/ or how to never sacrifice your dignity for any man ever?/ but you swallow the words/ like they are cacti dipped in honey/ they tear your throat/ but you don't want them to tear your home.

Heavy breaths/ dark room/ beneath the sheets lies one body/ alone/ a hand reaches out for the other/ but it's empty/ the only body wakes up/ and hears the loud breaths/ living room/ silent footfalls on the carpeted floor/ door creaks open/ there lays another body/ holding a screen to his face/ look closely/ naked women in different shapes and colours/ charcoal coloured device/ or a weapon in disguise/ a user can't differentiate/ sun fades away and the moon takes its place/ but the man's euphoria doesn't go away/ bare women inside the phone are held hostage/ guess it quenches the thirst for violence in a sadist's mind.

Fetishize my body until my soul snaps/ for I am a woman/ who deserves your sweet death/ govern every part of body/ 'cause what if I slip through your grip/ and become something more than what you think of me/ pierce my soul with your words/ then my body with your blood stained/ remorseless knives/ glorify the wounds you cause me/ then name it as another gift from pop culture/ for I am a woman/ whose existence is nothing/ but an empty vessel/ meant to be only full by/ the fear/ the hate/ the rules/ and the regulations/ that holy men deem fit to pour into my being/ for I am a woman/ and I don't deserve to breathe/ without a man's sinful attestation.

Male Gaze | Disapproving Parent's Gaze – Anushka (she/her)

Before you please a male's gaze, you cut parts of yourself for a disapproving parent's gaze.

He's on the phone, you're walking down the street, the streetlight catches a glimpse of you in his eyes and you try to run, run as fast as the wind walks on a casual November morning. But this is not a November morning, this is the 16th night of June, the hour hand isn't resting at 6, but rather resting at 2. You're late, too late to walk home alone, too late to reach home because your mom is still waiting with a disapproving look that'll greet you at the front door, the disapproving look that you could even hear in her voice when she demanded to know where you were.

Since the conversation with her on the phone you haven't been able to think straight, the noises grew louder and louder inside your head and right now when you are walking down the street while he's talking on the phone and watching your hurried steps, you can feel his eyes even though you haven't looked at him even once. You can feel his eyes touch parts of you that have no meaning in this life yet hold the very significance of your femininity. You try to adjust the way your body looks so you can disapprove of the male gaze that's maybe already disapproving of your body. You try to hide the pretty lines across your face and wear your best frown and even though it's dark, you want him to think that you're miserable enough, that you're going to bite his hands off & chew his fingers until they turn your teeth olive, but little does he know you won't do anything like that, this frown is a false spider's web which only ever swallows the one who stitches it across the whole town.

This is when the phone vibrates one last time before it switches off. Sweat beads collect around your neck and trace your spine as they leave. You know your mom well, you know she'll be calling again, and even though you are just a 5 minute distance from home, you need to pick the call up so she doesn't end up worrying about you. The man on the phone is trying to find a way to get closer to you but you have been walking as fast as the thoughts in your head. You can't help but compare him to her. The one time she looked down at your body and felt your chest protruding out like a rebel, the one time she called you a slut during an argument and you tried to ask her why she called you that and she looked into your eyes, shrugged and said "I never said that." And now you spend too much time trying to not look like a slut, trying to cut your body into pieces, trying to fit it in clothes that don't make your body look too feminine. But then there's a town you live in, a country you were birthed into, and a world that never accepted you that's stained with the crimson colour of a male's gaze and you realise no amount of cloth bras, round-necked dresses, or hurried steps can ever be enough to keep you safe.

Male gaze is similar to a disapproving parent's gaze. A disapproving parent's gaze is born out of years of internalised male gaze. Male gaze / Parent's gaze—both stain each other with quite the same amount of red.

In the Air (In the Teeth) – Pink Zombie Rose – Dia VanGunten (she/her) **& Beppi** (she/her)

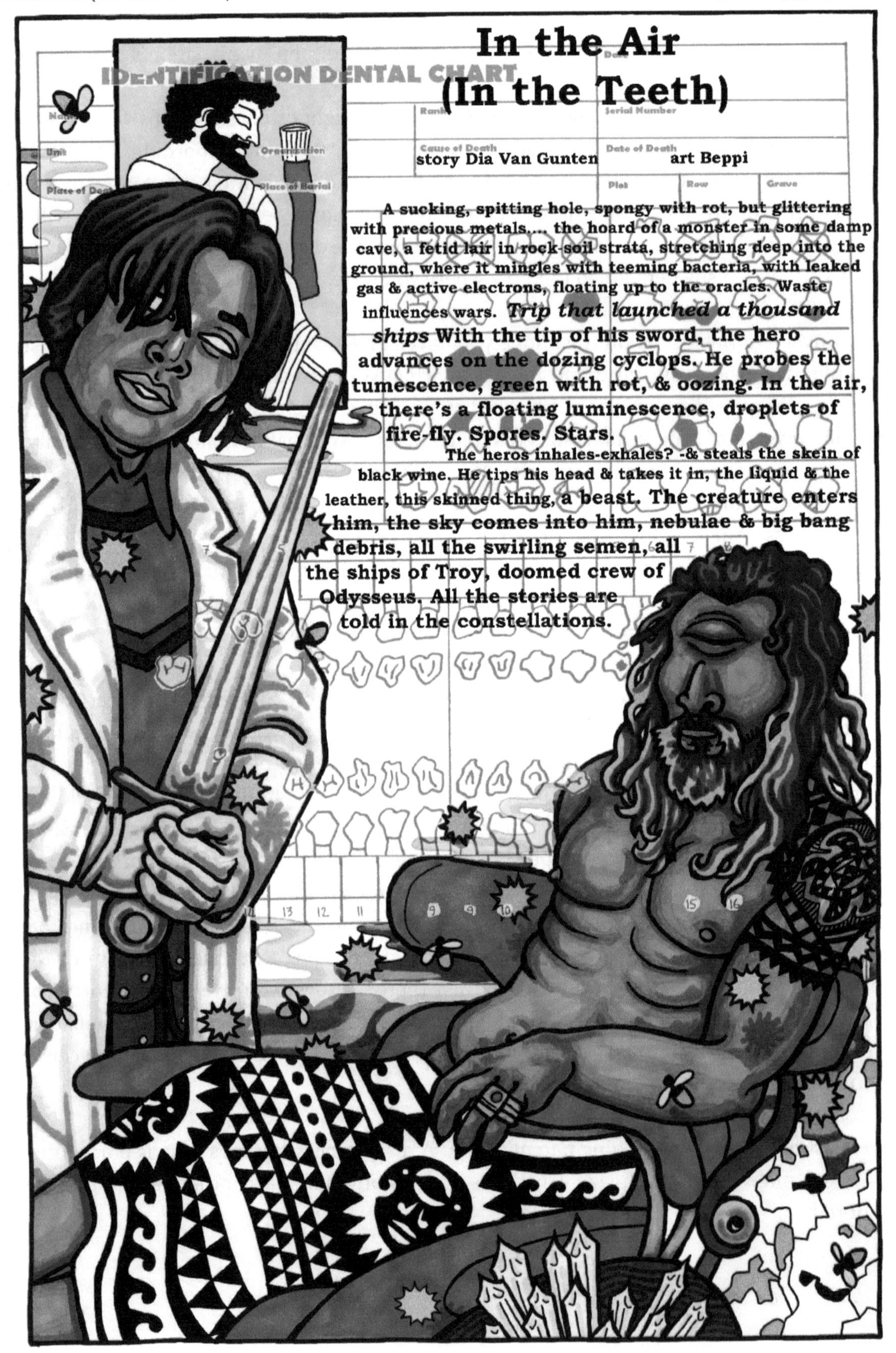

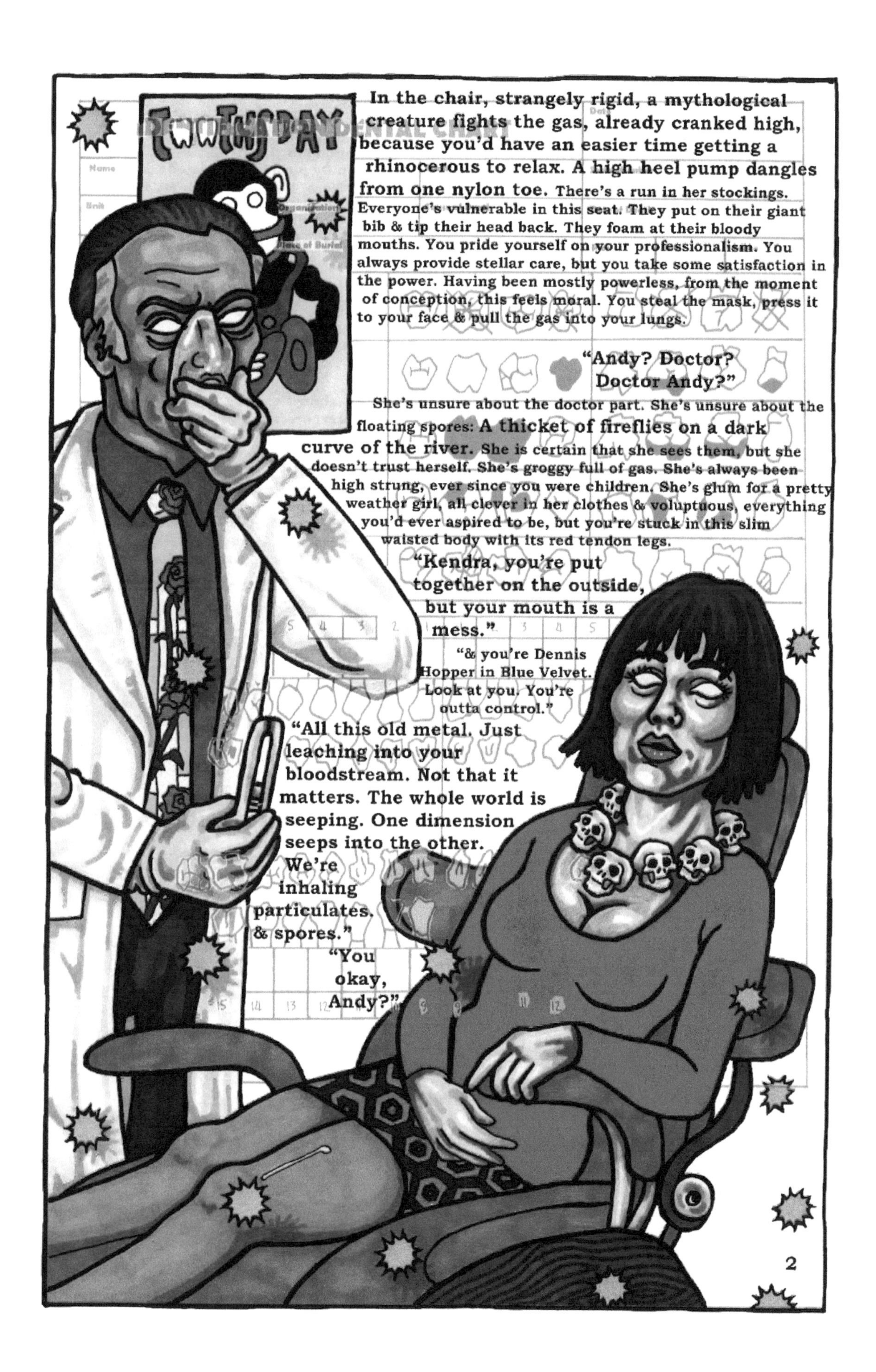

In the chair, strangely rigid, a mythological creature fights the gas, already cranked high, because you'd have an easier time getting a rhinocerous to relax. A high heel pump dangles from one nylon toe. There's a run in her stockings. Everyone's vulnerable in this seat. They put on their giant bib & tip their head back. They foam at their bloody mouths. You pride yourself on your professionalism. You always provide stellar care, but you take some satisfaction in the power. Having been mostly powerless, from the moment of conception, this feels moral. You steal the mask, press it to your face & pull the gas into your lungs.
"Andy? Doctor? Doctor Andy?"
She's unsure about the doctor part. She's unsure about the floating spores: A thicket of fireflies on a dark curve of the river. She is certain that she sees them, but she doesn't trust herself. She's groggy full of gas. She's always been high strung, ever since you were children. She's glum for a pretty weather girl, all clever in her clothes & voluptuous, everything you'd ever aspired to be, but you're stuck in this slim waisted body with its red tendon legs.
"Kendra, you're put together on the outside, but your mouth is a mess."
"& you're Dennis Hopper in Blue Velvet. Look at you. You're outta control."
"All this old metal. Just leaching into your bloodstream. Not that it matters. The whole world is seeping. One dimension seeps into the other. We're inhaling particulates, & spores."
"You okay, Andy?"
2

IDENTIFICATION DENTAL CHART
She discarded "doctor". It doesn't matter anymore, your job. The world is ending. You have zero faith in this undead apocalypse ever reversing course. You know better. You grew up with Dr. Zombie, head honcho of the ol' shit show. You've seen Aton meltdown over literally nothing- a twisted sock, a juice box- so you know he's no hero. He's no friend, either, but he's on your mind. You have moments of gasping lucidity, & you think,
"I should probably call that guy."
The Verne brothers. Yikes. They grew up to be a pair of pricks, but with perfect teeth. A marvel of orthodontics! In the 5th grade, they had a matching set of fangs that poked through their gums, high above the rest of their teeth, & pointy. Slick & gleaming. In the 6th grade, they were fitted for braces, & you watched as menacing magic was forced into alignment.
While it happened at almost exactly the same pace, there was a period of two weeks where you could tell one twin fom the other. It wouldn't be long before Atom was defanged, so you struck during the spring field trip. You lured him behind the dumpster at Brain Freeze. He & his brother had brand new, easter basket converse, so Atom refused to cross the puddle of melted strawberry ice cream, which merged with a sticky crust of cherries jubilee. It smelled like rancid grease, where they dumped the fry oil after so many batches. When Atom didn't want to come, you showed him your cock. It was nothing to see back then, but it got Atom's attention. Just the fact that you did it. *You.* The gangly tangle-tooth who collected calculators & did a wicked Steve Martin impression. You lift the nitrous mask.
"D'you still hang out with the twins?"
"We're adults now. No one hangs out."
"You still fuck the one?"
"Why? Do you need to see the doctor?"
3

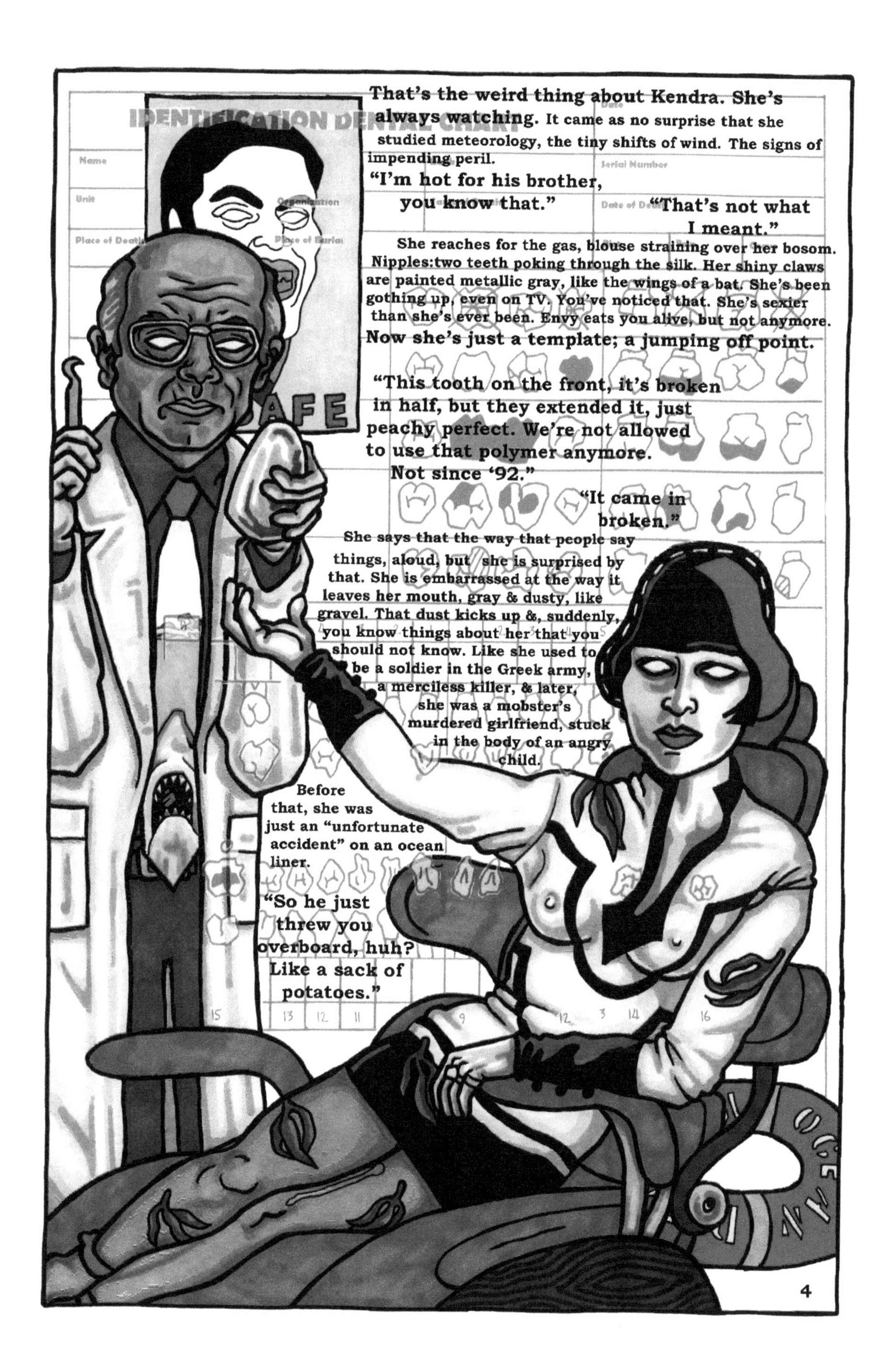
That's the weird thing about Kendra. She's always watching. It came as no surprise that she studied meteorology, the tiny shifts of wind. The signs of impending peril.
"I'm hot for his brother, you know that."
"That's not what I meant."
She reaches for the gas, blouse straining over her bosom. Nipples:two teeth poking through the silk. Her shiny claws are painted metallic gray, like the wings of a bat. She's been gothing up, even on TV. You've noticed that. She's sexier than she's ever been. Envy eats you alive, but not anymore.
Now she's just a template; a jumping off point.
"This tooth on the front, it's broken in half, but they extended it, just peachy perfect. We're not allowed to use that polymer anymore. Not since '92."
"It came in broken."
She says that the way that people say things, aloud, but she is surprised by that. She is embarrassed at the way it leaves her mouth, gray & dusty, like gravel. That dust kicks up &, suddenly, you know things about her that you should not know. Like she used to be a soldier in the Greek army, a merciless killer, & later, she was a mobster's murdered girlfriend, stuck in the body of an angry child.
Before that, she was just an "unfortunate accident" on an ocean liner.
"So he just threw you overboard, huh? Like a sack of potatoes."
4

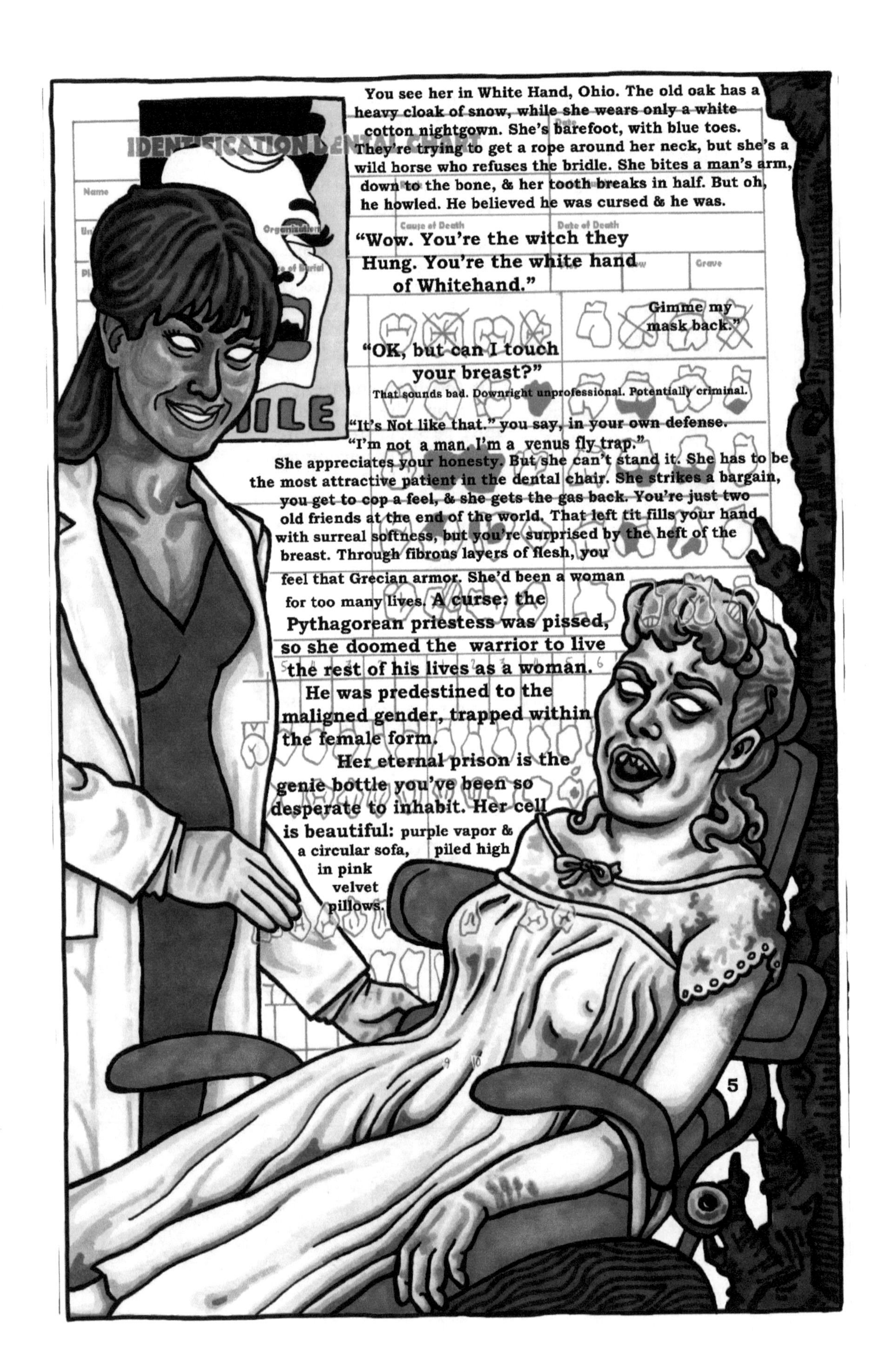
You see her in White Hand, Ohio. The old oak has a heavy cloak of snow, while she wears only a white cotton nightgown. She's barefoot, with blue toes. They're trying to get a rope around her neck, but she's a wild horse who refuses the bridle. She bites a man's arm, down to the bone, & her tooth breaks in half. But oh, he howled. He believed he was cursed & he was.
"Wow. You're the witch they Hung. You're the white hand of Whitehand."
Gimme my mask back."
"OK, but can I touch your breast?"
That sounds bad. Downright unprofessional. Potentially criminal.
"It's Not like that." you say, in your own defense. "I'm not a man. I'm a venus fly trap."
She appreciates your honesty. But she can't stand it. She has to be the most attractive patient in the dental chair. She strikes a bargain, you get to cop a feel, & she gets the gas back. You're just two old friends at the end of the world. That left tit fills your hand with surreal softness, but you're surprised by the heft of the breast. Through fibrous layers of flesh, you feel that Grecian armor. She'd been a woman for too many lives. A curse: the Pythagorean priestess was pissed, so she doomed the warrior to live the rest of his lives as a woman. He was predestined to the maligned gender, trapped within the female form.
Her eternal prison is the genie bottle you've been so desperate to inhabit. Her cell is beautiful: purple vapor & a circular sofa, piled high in pink velvet pillows.
IDENTIFICATION DENTAL CHART
5

Lipstick – Christina Lynn Lambert (she/her)

The kitchen wall remembers
an agreement
under duress
and what I had to give
to buy a chance
Under the paint
a hint of the stain remains
The scars we have to eat
twist our smiles a little

Four Pockets – Christina Lynn Lambert (she/her)

Give me four pockets

Let me hide my hands when they shake

That leaves two pockets for weapons

I'm a mouse that should run

A twig that can be snapped

But when the enforcers

come to silence my objections

I'm gonna keep my stubborn ass still

and scream until their ears ring

Even when I snap in their fists

I've got the weapons to be sure

my blood will burn

their reputations

Expanding the Now – Vita Lerman (she/her)

1.

She walks through words, watching them grow in neat rows, astonished at the early harvest. The weather cooperates, and she is grateful.

But she waits for more rain with some trepidation. It may or may not appear. Letting go is the only direction. In perseverance, in faith. Envisioning the pouring, the moist soil. The senses eager to emerge in new avatars. Lush and blooming.

2.

The rains come at night, concealing the moon. Bringing dreams of flowing lava. The distant island and its passions. The mountain thunders, erupting. Awakening the stars, witnessing their fiery passage across the skies. Marveling, transported, she remembers.

And words push through the fertile earth, seeking sunlight. Recalling all those falling drops of meaning, the nighttime wanderings, retold.

3.

She hears his words resounding in another tongue. The seeds of her creations. He is a master and she his disciple, growing her crops syllable by syllable, learning to listen for inner tones, playing with sound.

She learns to honor the earth as well, that silence, subterranean, profound. The pure potential beneath all knowing. She touches it, tenderly. Cultivates stillness. Expanding the now.

4.

Humble, she readies the ground for what is to follow. The encounter she so patiently awaits. The new green bursting out of the darkness. The leaves unfurling, revealing their stories. And later, flowers, opening, iridescent and glowing, whispering secrets to the wind.

She stands before this mystery of lifeforce brimming, in awestruck wonder. Finding her breath, her heartbeat pulsing with the rhythms newly formed. Discovering the melody, the harmonies. Rejoicing.

5.

And the rains return. Each drop a reflection, a tiny mirror of the world in all its manifestations. A teaching, wise counsel that she welcomes.

Her task is to choose, among the possibilities presented. Form, arrange meanings, images to make visible the hidden knowing. Intimations from the spirit realm.

6.

The blazing flames inform that knowing. The joining in all its candor. Purified by fire. Desire and more desire.

Her memories fuel the current burning. The before becomes the now.

7.

She wants to transmit that fire of the spirit. Each word, each phrase a spark that enters and transforms. The third eye opens, glimmers. Offers glimpses of the self arriving home, incandescent and restored. With tales that shimmer, visions wonderous to behold.

Her will is once more strong, aligned with nature's movements. As the now unfolds.

8.

The drumbeat sounds in the distance. The ritual dance begins anew. Calling the spirits to descend. To share their medicine, their stories.

She too dances with abandon, eyes half-closed, in a trance. Inviting inspiration.

9.

And when it strikes, she is prepared. The words she harvests ripe with dreams and memories, infused with elemental spirits. She bows in gratitude. Thanks the earth, the rains, the raging fire.

And the now that holds it all.

Cradling the Future – Vita Lerman (she/her)

1.

She carries the world of possibilities. Womb stretched, cradling the future. Caressed by the warm night. All around, the spirits swirl in anticipation. Whispering. Promising enchantment.

She is ready.

2.

In the tall grass she sits, communing with the moon reflected in the water. It is so close and she reaches out to touch the liquid light. It moves beneath her fingers, and she contemplates the shifting lunar phases until the pale round fullness is restored, stable once again.

3.

She allows the moon to enter, speak through her. Surrender to its wisdom, the greater knowing of that celestial wanderer. She is strong and can withstand the letting go of limiting perception. Allow expansion, the seeing with new eyes.

She is willing to create what is to come. To bear the newness yet unknown growing within her.

4.

She dreams and the full moon follows to that realm. She sees it glowing in her womb now, and her eyes too begin to glow, charged with wonder.

She hears a voice speaking of balance. Judgment and mercy, and the perpetual movement between those opposing pillars. She does not yet know, but she will.

5.

The drumbeat summons fire into being. The rebel flames are dancing with the wind. She listens as their fiery voices urge her to question the habits of the past, abandon the bounds of the present. To free her spirit and attune to the haunting melody within. To move according to its rhythm. To bring new life into the mystery unfolding.

6.

She remembers that night, the sultry air, the clear water mirroring the moon. The magic of its proximity. The touching. The entering her belly. The glow.

Reality or dream? Memory.

7.

And so from memory the future is created. Memory, where dualities merge. And manifest in radiant beginning.

The Siren – Vita Lerman (she/her)

1.

She is a creature of the sea and air. Uniting elements, embodied. Inhabits equally the turquoise waters and the purple skies. And loves the cliffs, the solitary island.

Her song is for herself.

2.

She basks in sunlight, dives into the depths. She knows beyond knowing the miracles of time. The ever-present now and all that it contains.

The transformations that it allows.

3.

And when she soars above the clouds, wings, multicolored, spreading wide, she is pure freedom. Pure abandon. Nourishing her eyes.

Her seeing manifests in sound. Strange melodies, perpetually evolving. Words flowing in a secret tongue.

4.

She brings these gifts back to the island. The cliffs, the wet sand, her captive audience. The wind carries echoes of her song.

That enter dreams of those who can hear.

Shapeshifters – Vita Lerman (she/her)

1.

A cloud leisurely extends into possibility. Exploring the periphery. An image forms almost. And just as gradually becomes another. Dissipates once more. Shifting, in slow motion, across the pale blue sky.

And thoughts too are evolving, pushing the boundaries of words. Leisurely, one shape begets another. Morphing, expanding meanings. Searching for resonance.

2.

When the sea god Proteus approaches, time stands still. The only motion is the waves. Flowing only in perception. Shape shifting. Knowing all. Eluding questions. Of time past and future. Only the now is to be revealed.

3.

And then there is light. Transforming everything it touches. Recalling each object to itself. Releasing hidden knowing. From the oblivion of darkness. Returning.

Altered, in the clarity of encounter.

The Tree Feeling of Life – Vita Lerman (she/her)

1.

She observes the silent dance, the tree, its limbs extending, curving. A gesture suspended mid-breath. Only on the surface. The movement continues, subtle. Completing itself, slowly, in her mind.

She is equally entranced by the visible motion, branches breathing with the wind. Engaging the world. Allowing. And then gracefully returning, resuming the stillness of the dance.

2.

She looks at the bark, how it bears the fingerprints of time, those patterns ancient with knowing. Growing from within. Keeping safe the precious moisture. The stories to be told. As the dance unfolds.

3.

She thinks of the roots, intertwining, reaching the depths. Communing with the rich soil, the mysteries beneath. Learning.

She too wants to connect that deeply to the living earth. To expand in the nourishing darkness, the origins of that sunlit dance.

4.

And when the new green bursts in spring, she wants to join the dance as well. Enraptured by that force that leaves her breathless.

She too follows the seasons. And now is the time of flow and feeling and creation. A celebration of pulsing continuity, in union with itself.

5.

The tree feeling of life, she says, to remember. Her mantra. Her inspiration. How many times it pulled her out of deep despair, that dark and narrow place that blinds and deafens. Into the light, and recollection of her self.

Memories rippling, reflecting green undulations. Sparkling. Playing. Restored.

"yes | and" – Megan Hatch (she/her)

The earth is burning, and not in a Paris sort of way.

We're told to lean in, only to find ourselves constantly leaning down

to pick up the pieces.

Losing ground, falling down.

The days are a cycling blur of need and numb, numb and need.

Paved paths lead to swift dead ends.

We cannot justify our way out of this.

It's time for abolition of the means and the end

of meanness.

Healing is happening.

We're here, we fear, yet we won't keep getting used to it.

We fall in, call in,

reach out and sometimes shout

with joy.

We mend the cracks with the gold we have, and that we are,

so we can carry water

and each other.

leaning in | falling down

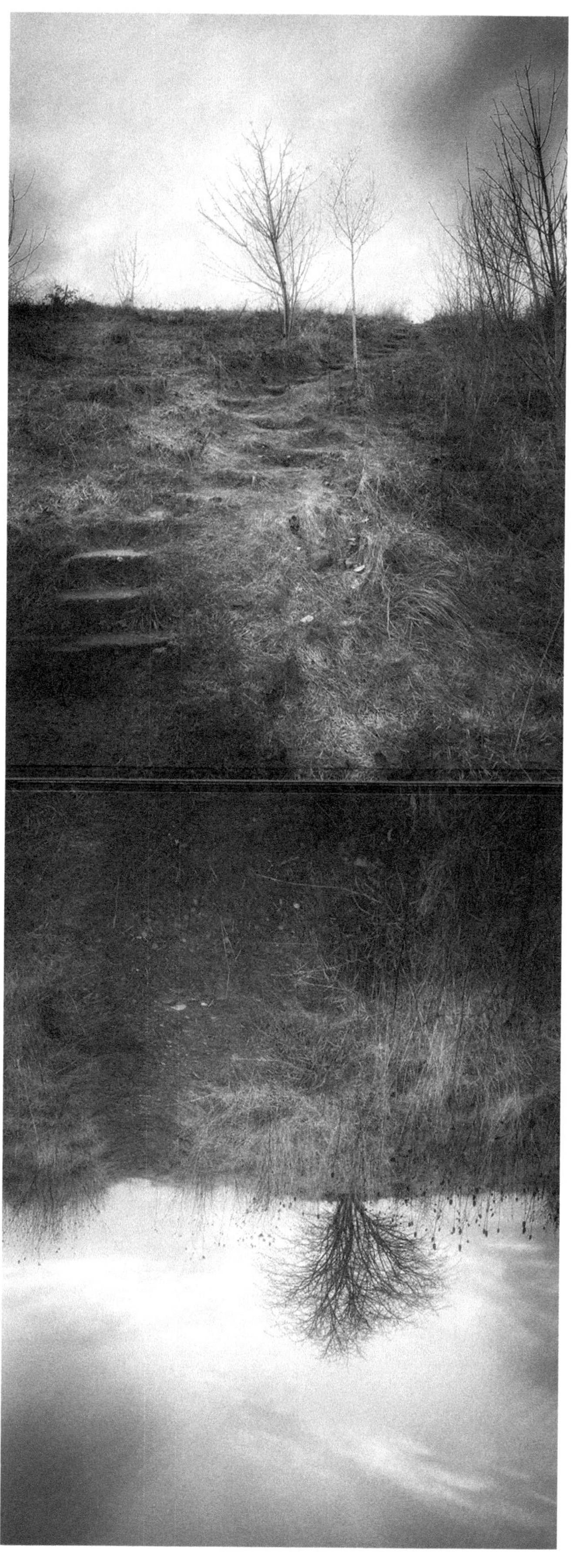

reaching | finding rest

the way isn't clear | here we are

almost there | losing ground

Corrido (Humming) – Kristin Lueke (she/her)

Ella me canta in murmurs,
hymns that I alone could carry—
Mijita, life exquisitely
will happen si amas sin temor.

Recuerda, si debes, debes
llorar sin vergüenza.
Your heart is yours to bear.
Deja quemar el mundo en ti.
A fist cannot carry ashes.

Mi linda, we are blessed to drift
through valleys como viento,
como ecos contra paredes de montañas.
You'll never need a man to tell you your name.
Nunca anclas, we are dust, my love
We rise—   spread—   vivimos en fuego

My hummingbird, quick-hearted, flame
a thousand miles from home, broke.
She feeds the earth.
Es la vida.
We struggle because we must.

Palomita, says my mother's mother
whose mouth I have forgotten,
Do not, I beg, *my love, forget*
these hands that have always held you.

First thing – Kristin Lueke (she/her)

to know i was not made by any man.

Unmade by any man, I am a caravan of unmothered mothers
reaching in the pre-dawn dark toward—if not safety—
anything else. Untethering from cruelty.

My grandmother left her home at seventeen, like my mother,
like me. Unmade by men and born to leave.

When I was five I met my grandmother's mother. She told me
I was cursed and she could tell by the fat pink strawberry tumor
my bottom lip bore since the day I was born. It stayed there
until I was old enough to think, from time to time,
I'd rather be dead than anything else. I'd rather be unmade.

Children aren't cruel because they're born that way.
My great-grandmother met a five-year old girl
and told her she was cursed. Placed all that heavy history
on my childish mouth. Compelled her daughter to leave
her home, having been unmade by a man who was dead
within the year. Called her daughter evil. Called me cursed.

I cut the strawberry from my lip.

Keep that memory in my mouth.

Leaving/home – Kristin Lueke (she/her)

I take to cursing early.
Believe I'm haunted.

Beg my body:
see me back.

I learn I bruise easy.
I think to me
who wants some?
I take what I can get.

I do not learn.
I try on woman,
try on women.
Learn this makes me
worth bruising.

I can not lose
what I never wanted.

Cut off all my hair, leave
a word like home.

It Spits You Out – Elaina Battista-Parsons (she/her)

Our Lady of the Laundry – Kristina Percy (she/her)

Here she is on nights you couldn't possibly cook another meal. Sunny afternoons she taps your shoulder in the garden: ten more minutes & you might've missed pickup, but she would never. She braids your daughter's hair in the morning, dishes still scraping the counter. Your daughter seems to hate it less, or at least there are fewer threats of cutting her curls. She drives all over town for kids' Tylenol; for that one LEGO set she knows is sold out, anyways. She'll listen to the same song all day if she has to and do it again tomorrow. She eats the leftovers. Hangs up everyone's towels. Drinks cold coffee without complaint.

She'll fuck your husband when you've had all the sticky fingers you can stomach. Hell, she'll fuck you on the couch when the kids are probably asleep & you are sitting alone for maybe the first time that day & when your husband asks, *Are you ready for bed?* you can tell him, *As soon as I fold this laundry, I'm coming.*

Checkup – Kristina Percy (she/her)

Six weeks
after my daughter is born my doctor asks:
How are you doing?

I didn't know there could be this much
laundry. Has it always been this loud?

Last week I stood in the kitchen,
watched the eggs burn. Yesterday
we fell asleep on the couch the way
you hear about babies suffocating
in the news. This morning she woke
at 3am, needing nothing, just
awake.

We leave the house every day.
That must be something.

Have you ever noticed how tiny
her wrists are in your fist? (No,
I suppose not.)

My jaw cracks
atop angry teeth:
Fine fine fine.

Sonnet for Boudica (sp?) – Kristina Percy (she/her)
"Dig uncovers Boudicca's brutal streak" — The Guardian, 03 December 2000

After the death of her husband, the rape
of her daughters, her own flesh stretched thin &

raw: is it any wonder Boudica
flayed each man she could lay her sword upon?

It took ten thousand of them to catch her.
Of course she poisoned herself not to chance

again a Roman groom; I would have too.
If mothers had been the ones to tell it,

speaking it into their wombs, their children's
hair, we might have known. But Dio, being

a man and also a scribe, writes it down
instead: letters shifting or lost; replaced;

a hundred generations live & die
before we learn *Boudica* means *the Queen*.

Last rites for my son – Kristina Percy (she/her)

I hope you are warm.

This small & distant
prayer. No one
even listening for it
yet.

I hope you are lying down, or perhaps
resting in a favourite chair. I hope
the lights are dim. Or maybe: tepid
sunshine, the kind that snags
on the air after a brief & fearsome
rain. You should have a glass of water,
a straw; that one pair of socks, loved
thin. Your nails are too long & I hope,
even after so many years of answering *why*,
they shine that same candid red. I hope
you can hear the quiet music of people
speaking low & sad but not ravaged:
let this be a song they've sung before. I hope
you are near a window, & outside a tree
shuffles gently in the breeze. I hope
you can imagine it still: that wind,
cool across your long & wearied
bones.

Surely even this
asks too much. How little
hope guarantees
a good life?

That there is more
of anything.
That you stay for all of it.
That an honest obituary would read,
I'm glad
I was here.

dear younger me – jai (they/them)

dear younger me,
i think about you all the time. you're me,
i'm you, we're each other,
i don't know you, i love you,
i'm proud of you for trying, i'm grateful
that you helped me get this far.

i think about when you tried on that word for the
first time;
wore it like a shirt covering your body, not too big,
not too small, just perfect.
how that same word was used against you,
against *me*,
and against your brothers and sisters
and siblings and friends like—
like it was a *curse*, and not the blessing
you didn't understand, back then.

i think about how you struggled and cried
and wept out your pain
and wished you were born *right*,
and wished you weren't *this*. i remember how you
wept and wept and wept and wept:
why am i like this? why am i wrong?

you thought about people who were killed
because of their love, their body,
their pride,
you thought about how
you're not allowed to *marry* in
one hundred and sixty
eight
out of one hundred and ninety
five
countries,
you thought about how people
ask you to choose and choose
when you're not pink or blue,
you're purple;
when you're not just one or the other,
but neither.

and you thought:
is this my future? is this what i am doomed
to be?

but you see,
younger me,
you were wrong. you were hurt
and you were scared and you thought you were
alone,
and you were wrong.

there are people out there
who saw your flag
and smiled,
there are people who held your
hands on the darkest nights,
there are writers and artists and singers and actors who told your story again
and again
and again,
because it was their story too.

we wept, and we wept, and we wept, trying to break free
of the chains of society
and a thousand hearts came to us,
coloured in the same hue as ours,
wiped away our tears, told us,
'you are not alone. you are not
broken, and you are *not* wrong.'

these are the shackles that
society has placed on us, the slurs and the
deaths and the laws,
and this is the key;
our community,
the flags we all keep,
the bonds we've formed together,
our hands linked, our words, whispering:
'you are whole. you are human.'

our story may be dark and painful,
younger me,
but it's a story of success,
of wars fought and won,
the story of halsey and emily dickinson,

lady gaga and freddie mercury, oscar wilde
and virginia woolf, elton john and walt whitman,
marsha p johnson and laxmi narayan tripathi,
and manvendra singh gohil and alan turing and sally ride and sylvia rivera and
a thousand other people,
real and made up, different
in so many ways,
but all
who are like us.

younger me, you know how
we've always hated chains and customs
and we've always loved rebelling?

society tells people like us to hate ourselves,
to be ashamed, to hang our head and love
someone we can't and be someone we
aren't—

i'll tell you this, society:
our fists gleam red with the blood of our enemies,
we stand strong on the foundation our family built before us,
the family that fought for our future,
the family that helped us understand that we are beautiful and whole and
human;
the family that gave us a home.
and we will keep fighting and shouting and screaming
and bleeding and you order us to hate ourselves,
but,
but,

we've always loved rebellions.
and i think the greatest rebellion
against society:
well, it's loving ourselves. because
we
are extraordinary

love,
jai

Untitled – Rachel Coyne (she/her)

Untitled – Rachel Coyne (she/her)

$5 Angel Wings – Mimi Flood (she/her)

My angel wings cost five dollars at a garage sale / held by glue and a safety pinned halo / walking across town with shoes in my hand and blisters on my feet / mouth filled with smoke / my skin is bad because it tells my truth / it has little seeds buried deep / blooming faster than your heart can beat.

Rosary Bead Eater – Mimi Flood (she/her)

Eater of rosary beads hanging from the branches of the trees. Sky of violets fluttering a heartbeat. Jewels falling crumbling into dust. A braid of roses down my throat. A watercolor between my thighs. I blur into you. Light and darkness leech onto my wrists like a vanilla perfume. It's my birth.

Who are you? – Mimi Flood (she/her)

Where I grew up I collected empty drug baggies left on the front steps and used them to gather my tears. One for heartbreak. One for a friendship ending. One for rejection. One for sadness. One for...

Write names on it after the people like an in memoriam at the Oscars. Roaches come during the night making shadow puppets on the walls and the baby mouse glued in the trap cries for its mother. My mother cried about not buying a birthday gift but the rent was due and that bill and this bill and this is going to be shut off for a while and we got to buy groceries for the week because all we do is live week to week. And all we think is why do we have to live like this while the landlord cashes in and school made me feel like a nobody. And nobody could hear me scream. Nobody could see the blood dripping from my wrist. I once read an Emily Dickenson poem and it said *I'm nobody. Who are you? Are you nobody too?* And it took me the longest time to even think that I was somebody. Now, who are you?

Bulimia of a Fat Girl – Mimi Flood (she/her)

They say when you fall down you can get back up again / but the safety net on the bathroom floor where I binged and purged seems to suffice / I have a pizza box with the crusts left / half a bag of potato chips / two big kit kats / endless scrolling of Instagram and 45 tabs open of how to be no longer fat and lose weight / a toilet bowl filled with my last meal. I get the anxiety of eating in public / so I go on the treadmill an extra 45 mins / I haven't lost weight / so it's easy to be bulimic when you're fat / And someone always asks did you eat / and you binge when you're bored / binge when you're sad / binge when that shows comes on / and your doctor always weighs you and asks do you exercise / gives you compression socks for the swelling at your ankles / says your blood pressure is high / and a lover squeezes your stomach / and a lover wants to take your shirt off /and a lover tells you they love you / I know I'm nothing more than human. / body / skin / scars / bone / cellulite / veins / hair / breast / hips / fat / joy/ judgement / I don't want to be sorry for it anymore / I don't want to feel bad for it anymore.

Nosebleed – Mimi Flood (she/her)

A body is a birthday gift with a name and my vagina is owned by the government. You want a gospel in the back of my throat with no panties on. You want a rare girl. You want that perversion of a quiet girl. That hush hush. Call me baby and then the next a bitch. A Cool girl. A Doe eyed girl. An Angel girl. I bandage my knuckles but nothing feels sorrow but the lines on my palms that filled with tears. You would look for a heartbeat in a uterus before you would look for a rapist. The girl is raped. The girl is beaten. The girl is dead. But what was she wearing? I have an ode to a mad girl she pops and sizzles and sheds. A lobotomized girl. A nameless girl. A burned girl. They act like they want you, even love you, but most can't even say vagina. Call it the thing. Girl parts. Pink center. Jelly. Too much? But they can't wait to fuck you. I'm a godless girl. Purgatory girl. Girl in limbo. Girl with a nosebleed.

Anatomy of an Orchard – Cheryl Tan (she/her)

Rind

When you eat red fruit you start with your teeth, top to bottom, scrape wax off the freshness of skin. Whitened grease, like gloss varnish. Fast forward till tomorrow. As a kid your idols were Strawberry Shortcake and Winx Club. As a teen it was Marina and the Diamonds. Drip. Your cheongsam flutters away on its polyester wings. Drip. Adam was just as tempted as Eve. Drip. You were raised in a house where men beat and women weep. You will not be the one who is weeping.

Flesh

Bad apple song like a bullet hell track. Tokyo-US paraphernalia. Asian *gyarus* with bleached hair and highlights. J-Pop girl crush apathy. The two nerds at the back of your class have started dating. You might just rot from jealousy. At the height of your vanity you score through the shelves of the nearest Lovisa, spin the display racks until they blur, lift up an earring and the magic of it erupts, spills out, wraps itself inside you. Fairytale towers, capitalist queens. Snow White was never this easy to read.

Core

There's an eighty-year-old who stopped growing at eight because she'd worked herself into the home, bless her. Two inches to the cupboard, three inches to the pot and over four decades to the chimney. No scepter for her slavery. Rosy red-capped ordinance workers. The Soviet working dam. Suffrage comes from leaflets dropped in forests of starving women, from 1950s trad wife mags. What else would you expect within this country? Pink ladies shield their seedlings from the amber slight of rain. Every part of you is on fire.

Seed

Drink the girl within the cider and call it delicious. Dig the dirt within the flesh and call it divine. Take your dresses and your dolls and drag them out sweetly, like crisp julienned peels, spirals of red pericarp. You can't tell knives from cooking apples. Dessert girls. Jilted girls. Bittersharp deserted girls. Girls like metaphors of flower and fruit. Your mama hates your *lao lao* and your *lao lao* hates the world for giving her ideas too late. Down here you are untouchable and bleeding.

Sprout

There's a child inside you picking pockets full of posies, stuffing them where flowers shouldn't go. There's a boy who is wanting and waiting for you. You're not sure if you want him just yet. It's the season of blossoms now, where every tree breaks on the cusp of ripe juice, bends its boughs to kiss the ground. Amen. Anything you plant will grow into the sun, so you kneel, eyes closed, not for god nor for man but for yourself, O precious pip in the orchard. You were built entirely on love. You *will* keep on loving.

Lady Bone Demon orders her next meal – Cheryl Tan (she/her)

i think i'll go for the petrified monk / thanks / yes i want him medium rare / how i love a felled immortal / for drinks i'll have the heavenly peach juice (sparkling) / make it a meal combo please / this necklace i bought from The Jade Emporium / it's like *taobao* but slightly better / haggled with princess iron fan for it / nearly got blown off the edge of the earth / this is a charming establishment / curtains purer than lotus leaves / i can almost taste it / how long has it been since i've loved a soft being / someday my mouth will remember to eat / crunch down on skeletal shards of my name / *bai* like dead poets blanched in moonlight / *gu* like the marrow of sick children's teeth / *jing* like monster witch / either sex preferable / a monkey king used to come date me on Sundays / he'd order repentance and false chivalry / on some days i put my bone hand on my cheek / pretend he is still there holding me / *bai gu jing* / white bone spirit / do you accept tips in ashes / remember the monk that i told you about / make sure to cook his past lives out of him / make him as tender as cygnets in spring / i don't want to wash myself after i eat

Dear Delilah – Cheryl Tan (she/her)

Shanghai 1930

Still got the talisman you gave me last year, the red cloth one with elaborate knots. *Shuangxi*[1]. Double happiness. What's it like in America, love? I bet you're being all fancy with the ladies and dashing gentlemen in their long dark trousers. I bet you fit right in with them. The thought of that makes me smile. The face powder you gave me has served me very well. You'll be surprised when you come back. I am now ten times prettier thanks to you.

A-Niang[2] let me bob my hair today—I'm a real modern woman now. It'll be funny to imagine it on your end, right? Delilah? Delilah with a D and an E and an AH. I am in love with all the letters of your name. They won't let me learn English but I'm secretly learning it from the ambassador next door, the one you said was too bookish for anything outside school. He looks slightly better now that he's married. His wife is a real piece of work but she makes the best fried lotus root in the country. I wish you were here to share it with me.

The pork rib soup business is doing well; *A-Die*[3] thinks we should expand into Europe. I support him in whatever he does. He says I am to be wed soon, for it was written in the stars. I refuse to believe anything can be written in the stars unless it is between you and me. That night when you kissed me behind the shophouse and there was dust everywhere, scattered like pieces of the moon. Your blond hair in my eyes and my neck. Our hearts breathing as one. You told me you wanted to show me the world. I believe you.

America, *mei guo*[4], the most beautiful country. *A-Niang* says I'll have to forget about you but I'm not doing it ever ever ever, not even when they break my toes so I'll never dance again. *Shuangxi*. Double happiness. Lilah, are you sure you still want to marry me? Are you going to come back from New York City and whisk me away with your fashionable heels and tassels? Either way I'm going to find a way to reach you. Do you hear me, Delilah Jane Pinkerton? I'm finding a way to reach you! No idea when I'll be there, but I will.

Love you always,

Jiang Mengying
(江梦莹)

---

[1] *Shuangxi (双喜)*: Literally "double happiness", it is used as a decorative symbol of marriage.

[2] *A-Niang (阿娘)*: The traditional address for "Mother" in Mandarin.

[3] *A-Die (阿爹)*: The traditional address for "Father" in Mandarin.

[4] *mei guo (美国)*: Literally "beautiful country", it means "America" in Mandarin.

Cheer – Raegen Pietrucha (she/her)

The only words I feel safe speaking I scream
alongside a team, combining them
with sharp chops and kicks, a killer

smile. Eleven girls and I devote
our weekdays to memorizing litanies
of victory, and our boys spring higher

each year as if our words
are manna. Atop the pyramid, held
like a house on a rock, my faith

never wavers; I feel the girls' mass
will always lift me as it does the team—
soaring, however briefly,

above enemies—undefeated,
untouchable, immaculate. And on the weekends,
when I can manage to get away from him, I run far

past the fence out back, hide my practice—
a zealot casting spells—hoping the right
words paired with the right actions will someday

help me take some form of flight—
recalling perfectly the patterns and tracts—
vital when you're the only one

who's coming to your defense.

*Originally published in *Euphony* and appears in Pietrucha's collection *Head of a Gorgon*

Sea Cleaving – Raegen Pietrucha (she/her)

The men of nets
have their ways. Wives
and daughters play their part, weave

so husbands and sons can leave
at dawn, sweep salted waters with lengths
of trains that callus their hands.

Poverty is obvious. It's the crisp of skin
peeling off the sunburned leather
of a sea-weathered neck. The stink of fish too deep

beneath the nails to be breached. The way
captives will always be clubbed in their traps
as if all smaller creatures were made simply

to pay a penance—the flimsy body buckling,
conferring blood, delivering one last
flail after the strike that finally breaks it

arrives. There is hunger—too much hunger.
Who knows where it comes from.
The day you meet him, your insides grind against

themselves; he lumbers under a palpable
weight of fish from that water—
wet, iridescent prizes glistening.

You pray they'll crush you.
They will. The moment your teeth gnash
meat, you christen him your lord.

*Originally published in *Paper Nautilus* and appears in Pietrucha's collection *Head of a Gorgon*

Mumfish – Raegen Pietrucha (she/her)

Mother, why didn't you protect your daughter?
I told you about the beast so long ago
but struggled alone under the weight of his water.

When he invaded my borders,
you pretended it was nothing, muffled his name in a bubble.
Mother, why didn't you protect your daughter?

Did you do it to retain some type of order
for the low, low cost of a good you thought expendable?
I flailed under the weight of his water

as if it were burial—which I suppose is called for
when the smallest snag can make great yarns unravel.
But, Mother, why didn't you protect your daughter?

A parent (and a woman too) could've easily ended the torture,
broken the tides that would follow. The irony here is less than subtle.
I nearly drowned under the weight of his water,

unarmed, unable to swim from the slaughter.
Sometimes I wonder if you would've missed me at all.
Mother, I'll never know why you didn't protect your daughter.

I'm still searching for a way through the weight of that water.

*Originally published in Pietrucha's chapbook, *An Animal I Can't Name*,
and appears in Pietrucha's full-length collection, *Head of a Gorgon*

Justice Isn't Possible: Why I Write – Raegen Pietrucha (she/her)

I watch a lot of true-crime shows: "Forensic Files," "Dateline," "Deadly" anything. And one thing, amid all the grizzly horrors some human has inflicted upon another, always strikes me—not due to its surprising or particularly revelatory nature, but because of its predictability.

When a surviving family member or friend of, say, a murder victim comments—usually after some guilty verdict has been rendered, before the screen fades to black—the survivors almost always say some version of this: "Although it doesn't bring my loved one back, I'm glad this person is unable to hurt someone else." The words tremble from jowls worn down into frowns of permanent grief, the eyes tired and swollen from saltwater surges.

It doesn't bring my loved one back. I return to this thought often when I think of my writing, my life, injustices endured.

I'm not here to argue whether America's justice system is just or actually does the job of imparting justice. I'm also not here to argue in favor of other justice systems, the old eye-for-an-eye deal or otherwise.

No. I am here to sit with this thought of things that, once taken, can never be returned to us—how much in life, once done, can never be undone. Life is not a document on a computer screen, a keyboard with a delete button. It is not a rough draft. It is, immediately, each second, the final and only draft of the story of one's life. If your eye is taken, taking the eye of the person who stole yours doesn't return your eye to you.

This doesn't mean we should let this lull us toward inaction and let wrongdoers continue harming others. Whenever we can, we must at least try to ensure that these people are unable to hurt someone else. That much, at least, is possible.

But what doesn't seem possible to me is justice. If we define the term as a sort of "making whole" once more of a person or people harmed, it is a thing the human brain can conceive of and the human heart may long for. But that doesn't make it a thing that exists.

This being said, the further a person is in their own existence from a certain type of body—namely, a white, cisgender, heterosexual male body—the further that person will likely find themself from being able to experience the type of "justice" some legal systems are able to offer. The #MeToo movement has highlighted what many survivors of sexual violence already knew: It is extremely difficult to obtain justice in the form of a conviction against a sexual predator.

According to the National Sexual Violence Resource Center, 1 in 5 American women will experience attempted or completed rape; in 2018, only 25% of those incidents were reported to police. More generally speaking, of incidents reported, less than 6% result in arrest, and less than 1% result in a conviction, according to The Washington Post. And the median length of convictions is two years, according to RAINN, with 60% rearrested for committing new crimes—sexual or otherwise—within three years of the original conviction. None of these statistics speak much to the sex crimes for which a statute of limitations has expired.

*

When I drafted my first poem about Medusa in 2007—my second semester in graduate school, working toward my MFA—survival of another kind was on my mind. My mother had battled breast cancer and won, yet I had come to notice since her double mastectomy something unjust about the way some men perceived and treated women like her who'd survived such tragedy—something that, for whatever reason, recalled to mind that mythic woman with snakes for hair, that body transformed into something considered so terrifying, it turned anyone who looked upon it to stone.

But as I delved deeper into the myth—or, more to the point, the myriad variations of the myth—I moved away from that idea and toward what, to me, is the real crux of Medusa's story: She is a woman who, in many versions of the myth, is raped by Poseidon on the altar of Athena; then, as if that wasn't heinous enough, she is transformed into a monster by Athena, who, it would seem, holds Medusa, not Poseidon, responsible for the crime that occurred. Medusa is a woman doubly punished, by man and woman alike, robbed multiple times over of any form of justice.

"But she can turn people to stone," you might say. "Isn't that some kind of justice she can wield against others?" I would argue, as I do in my poem "Relics" from my collection *Head of a Gorgon*, that it is merely a substitute, at best. And while Medusa possesses a supernatural power others do not, power and justice are, in the end, two different things.

*

I didn't come to grad school with some grand plan to write the great American poetry collection, whatever that would even be or be about. And even after I'd realized that, for whatever reason, this Medusa thesis was something I needed to write, I really couldn't articulate why.

In Medusa, I saw so many women I knew. Women from movies like "The Accused," "Delores Claiborne," and more. But also a loved one who was abused as a child; that predator got away with it. Another who was raped by multiple men in a single night; those predators, too, were never charged. And another who was assaulted as a child and assaulted later as an adult; still more predators walking free. And then there was me.

The last day of workshop, my thesis advisor and our class of five were hanging out in my apartment, stuffed full of pasta I'd made to celebrate the occasion. But after reading and discussing the last round of poems we would ever share together, my advisor turned to me, her blue eyes twinkling with that mischievous, inspired sparkle I'd come to know well during our program to mean she'd had some sort of epiphany, and she dropped the key to a queendom in my hands: "What if you brought these personal poems you've been working on together with the Medusa material and interwove them into a single story?"

I hadn't stopped writing poems about what I considered then to be non-Medusa things, including some things that had happened during my childhood, a combination of clear memories and an indistinct knowledge that haunted me from before a time I could even remember having acquired it, kind of like knowing how to walk but not being able to remember when or how I learned to. And the Medusa work, at that point, had focused on her adulthood, which is really all we hear about in the best-known tellings.

I was willing to bring the two together, but it would mean a reimagining of both sides of the equation. Medusa could no longer be someone separate from me. She had to fully enter my world; I had to open the door, look her in the eye unflinchingly, and embrace her here.

*

I was grateful for the elective component my MFA program built into our degree requirements. It was a welcome relief, in many ways, from writing, editing writing, talking about writing, reading more creative writing...

I chose a feminist theory class, which surprised no one who knew thing one about me, but it was curious to me, at least, that it had taken me so long to finally get into this type of women's studies course.

Among the many texts we read was Helene Cixous' "The Laugh of the Medusa." Of course, this text is widely taught and well-known, but at the time, I interpreted it as another sign from the universe that I was moving in the right direction, chasing this Medusa who'd been elusive but ever-present in my mind since that initial poem draft about her inspired by my mother's illness.

Looking back now, upon recently revisiting Cixous' piece, there was quite a bit that, admittedly, went over my head. I wasn't yet the person I needed to be to more deeply understand the text—much like, I came to realize only years after graduating from my MFA program, I was not the person then that I needed to be to write the Medusa book that sought to be written. That part of my education, my self-awareness, was not yet complete.

Still, there was something intriguing about Cixous' bold proclamation: "You only have to look at the Medusa straight on to see her. And she's not deadly. She's beautiful and she's laughing."

I wasn't sure I quite bought into that; Medusa, to me, was brimming with a righteous and quite justified rage at the injustices dispensed upon her—though that rage could be seen, from a feminist perspective, as beautiful. But I did agree with one of the earliest statements in Cixous' piece: "Woman must write her self: must write about women and bring women to writing, from which they have been driven away as violently as from their bodies—for the same reason, by the same law, with the same fatal goal."

Unsurprisingly, my work has generally not received the warmest reception from male writers. This is, in fact, why, before I applied to graduate programs, I specifically sought out only those universities that had at least one female faculty on staff—ideally, many more. I ended up somewhere that had two, and my work was still subject to the same tired feedback from some male professors and colleagues.

If you're a female writer reading this, you likely know the drill—along with some of the coded labels workshop misogynists employ to degrade us and our writing without specifically identifying the feminine and/or feminist aspects they find revolting: Domestic. Confessional. Unrelatable. Blah, blah, blah.

Much like a survivor's traumatic experiences can drive them away from their body, long to disassociate from or discard it in a vain attempt to simultaneously discard the violence that harmed the body, mind, and spirit, I could sense these men trying to drive me away from writing, from this new body I sought and was creating, instinctively, to take refuge in.

I'm grateful to Medusa for lending me her strength. Too many women—too many survivors—have been silenced already.

*

I haven't always had a strong sense of why I've been drawn to writing. I read a lot of books as a kid, I often tell people who need a quick and easy explanation, and that's true. It's also true that writing seemed to come naturally to me. A lot of writers—myself included—like to say our drive to write is about some sense of urgency; that too, for me, at least in part, is true. There is urgency to the story I'm sharing in *Head of a Gorgon.* It, like each and every survivor story, needs to be heard.

But the more I worked on the manuscript, the more Medusa revealed a deeper reason to me; her voice now was more than just the whisper it had been when I first heard her call.

She too knew what I knew: that justice for us would always be impossible. There is nothing any legal system can provide survivors that deletes—like writers delete unnecessary elements from their stories—what the body has suffered, what it became because of that suffering.

But in telling this story, in using our voices, there could be reclamation. There could be, as I strive to accomplish in a 14-part poem sequence in *Head of a Gorgon*, reinvention.

Or, as Cixous said, "She gives that there may be life, thought, transformation."

No, it doesn't bring my loved one back—the girl unharmed. Nothing can. Justice isn't possible. Instead, through writing, I am delivered another one that, if only I am brave enough to embrace her—woundedness and all—I can still, perhaps even more fiercely, love.

*This companion essay for Pietrucha's collection *Head of a Gorgon* was originally published in *Eunoia Review*

(Wo)(man)nequins – Raegen Pietrucha (she/her)

Work – Lydia Fern (she/her)

The damage dealt and sustained within our bones

Is the first pair of eyes on my work

I can't say "pray" without the damage in my bones

Suggesting to me you'll first hear "Jesus"

And maybe stop to wonder, "Is that not what she meant?"

In order for the work to lose the message it never had

You must create your own work

The strain and the quest, "Have I made an assumption?"

I ask you to heal as you read

A tremendous ask,

  on my part

But I don't ask you lightly

I don't ask you from The Other Side

Your

  health is nonbinary, not an unflipped lid nor a reachable destination

My

  healing is a state of Being,

But I ask you to interrupt that assumption:

  that Being is static completion

  that a healed human is a switch finally flipped

I ask you to close your eyes, and to watch the light behind your shell

I ask you,

  is it still? (an unmoving mass, destined to be only one thing forever, trapped and alone)

or

  is it a state of motion? (color and sparks, blending, unending, life in photokinetic change)

I ask you,

  does it stay the same no matter where you are?

or

  does it change when you move around?

We create a set of habits that we call "Myself"

And we don't watch the way we change every day,

or we dread it

To the assumption,

Motion is a grave threat

To the habit,

Healing is a worst fear

So when I ask you to move,

When I ask you to heal,

I know I threaten the storm clouds you've gathered as a buffer, the electric veil you inhabit as a hiding place

In the end I know no one can move you but you

And so I move only myself,

And I ask

Someone told him – Lydia Fern (she/her)

Someone told him

creation

is nothing but reshaping

the secret to creation lurks between disassembled pieces,

originality is dead,

so he falls apart

to create His Masterpiece

As a baby,
his eyes were wide, taking in light as it comes, and he was filled with wonder, but

also

with

fear

As a baby,
all that was left for him was to consume, his only cry for help a desperate wail for survival,
unmodulated and unrefined,
His creation was a piercing scream

for help

But something curious
happens to babies
raised in power culture
taught the Universal Truths are:

might makes right

creation mandates destruction

all that matters is you

the victor is written by his story

to love is to fight,

in a fight you must

WIN AT ALL COSTS

The baby grows to be a boy,
under abuse and presupposition that he's
riding the conveyor belt to hell
Pastor says "Love" as he beats his daughter, and takes her bedroom door away,
And the boy learns from this,

Love is Pain
Creation is Destruction
To Move Up, Punch Down

But that's what his 20s are for, he's assured
Mistakes and rage,
The brutal thrashing of feet to escape this one-way chasm

What he finds in his 20s
is unbridled isolation
he treats each moment as a war and wonders what about him makes her so uncomfortable
But he already learned,

If you're not with me, you're against me Every problem has a simple solution

destined
He is to fill someone's bed
programmed
entitled

No matter what, the problem is not him,

because he's only special

No amount of rebellion can take away his right to power,
after all:
The Gods depend on Man, Thus Man is God,
And what is he but Man? It's all he's permitted, but he's sure
His Masterpiece is waiting in there somewhere

As a God,

his eyes are wide, taking in the light of the flames he's lit, and he is filled with wonder,

also

with

fear

The corpses strewn before him,

"art is subjective" and a sour grin, a hoarse, chuckle

wheezing

The stranger's intestinal blood

he wears around his gaping mouth,

horror

the thrumming in the raging red ring

paranoia

regret

around his pupils

His scream rattles against the ceiling and the floor, manic and feral, as he rips and destroys,

seeking

His

Masterpiece

Do I Miss You – Caspian (he/him)

Mother of Demons – Veronica Szymankiewicz (she/her)

Mother of deadly sins and demons, wearing unholy grins,
birthing all dark things that occupy monstrous skins.
The forgotten wife of Adam bowed to no man and was cast out,
Eden's rules separate staunch believers from those who dare to question or doubt.
There is no place for insubordination,
when the goal is complacent subjugation.
Vilified as a femme fatale and an unspeakable abomination,
if she was created in God's image,
wasn't she a perfect creation?
Divine feminine who stood her ground,
seen as calculating and deceptive,
simply because she refused to be blissfully receptive and denounced a problematic perspective.
Women who do not fall in line and do as they are told,
are punished for being bold because there are appearances and inflated egos to uphold.
Banished to live as the Underworld's reigning queen,
she holds dominion over the biblically unclean.
Feared and abhorred for honoring her beauty and sensuality,
she is yet another casualty of projected inadequacy and unbridled audacity.
Her autonomy was labeled evil,
a tale as old as time, bordering on primeval.
Carefully molded from the same clay as her husband, she was his equal in all ways,
however, Lilith was literally demonized throughout history and mythology for setting her oppressive world ablaze.
Vicious smear campaigns where her name was dragged through the mud,
serve as a warning to women who have rebellion coursing through their blood.
Submit and be dutiful, as well as unquestioningly obedient,
or risk being classified as a disgusting whore and a child eating social deviant.
She is the genuine archetypal feminine, representing those who unabashedly claim their sacred power,
knowing in their souls they weren't made to be kept prisoner in an ivory tower or to grovel and cower.
How interesting that she became a villain for not backing down,
so Eve was created from lonely Adam's rib and given Lilith's rightful crown.
Poor Eve, blamed for the great fall from grace and ultimate expulsion from the Garden,
a mistake so grievous, eons later she is still unable to receive a pardon.
One woman carrying the mantle of blasphemous temptress and one, the easily tempted,
it's as if all women were doomed to fail by design regardless of which road is taken and what actions are attempted.
There is no way to win when men are in charge of the spin,
it makes you wonder who was actually responsible for committing the original sin.

Omniscient Celestial Friend – Marsha Meyers (they/them)

I traded God for the moon,
and saints for my deck of significators.
The guilt I shouldered into anxiety,
my bedtime prayers turned to clockwise movements,
and roadside incantations.
I traded god for the moon but kept
the altered spaces;
a wooden heart flush against the wall with a candle caged and a crown of incense,
a wicker dresser with a gaping mouth—exhaling green silks,
and a retired blue trunk holding suitcases stagnant.
I traded god for the moon and fell
to sleep again before noon,
without washing my face or saying grace, I made a meal and enjoyed it too.
I traded god for the moon and found
purgatory buried beneath saturn's meadow,
emptying its residence atop an eastern wave.
(the legend of heaven and hell are unrecognizable at this dream's pace.)
I traded god for the moon and melted
into blood...
flowing from a bugle's song for hours upon days.
I traded god for the moon and soon
weeks passed and the blood turned thicker—stopping the sea-goat's chant;
"leave us here beneath this spell
incant your magic above thy shell
encourage a feast shared by all
and understand this divine call."
I traded god for a penpal and their name is the Moon;
Titan,
Mimas,
and Rhea.
We speak each month.

Sun Spooked – Marsha Meyers (they/them)

When I rise with the Sun
my skin stains His smile
above me;
a reminder of His gaze,
the ceiling tiptoed in prints.

Lock the door.

When I rise with the Sun
my eyes peel apart
above me;
His dance refracts,
a performance in the shadows looming.

Check the blinds.

When I rise with the Sun
my peace permeated
above me;
He is a voyeur,
a-top my perch.

Do not make eye contact, you are not welcome here.

With the flood of light
He is a warrior;
Slicing through the window,
Swinging from one mirror,
He watches you begin the day again.

Let him look.

While I sit in the balance
Between the force, the pull, the push,
the protection of His cheshire.

You are not welcome here.

Toothy and teasing, His
voice drags on spirits wrapped
around a grid meant to protect

You are not welcome here.

catapulted towards the same reflection,
fractured at a slightly different angle.
the performance is desired not the watchful refraction.
Before the performance begins, please stop,

You are not welcome here anymore.

I built it I broke it – Marsha Meyers (they/them)

Darling,
I would be nervous to deny a connection
with snarled smiles tangled in contemplation,
Darling, incongruent to themself.

Incongruent to themselves.

Joy to leave the warmth
Power tied to a hilarious proposition.
Darling please don't leave the warmth of the bed!

a partner!

but a posey?

dolphins take on waves in confident pods of silly chatter,
Couch caves in front of treadmills in a nuclear family structure.

Darling, does your dad need it?
Need not be nine, but add thirteen.

a sandwich?

the remote?

the audacity,
I do not foresee,
routines of chatter up my ears through the back door.
crawled up and past the budweiser.
nor gossip nor worry, Darling. Stick it in your mouth and forget,
being left out of a joke.

eat an orange around four
but sleep comes even faster when I have rinsed my manifesto in yours.

I belong to her but she belongs to him.

Darling, I watched my fingers default to instagram.
Watched, Darling
just as I stared at your location.

Just as,
Handled raw tended to melt—
tips of my toes every morning, Darling,

I heard your door open.
I refused to fill the echo of silence.

Darling, crushed under green velvet—
hoping you'd break down the apartment doors.
Take off your shoes, Darling—
rest your feet on the backs of mine
balance on my stegosaurus spine,
stay tender as you boil a pot of noodle soup,

Just as your mother made,

but only as the Dallas heat subsided did I keep my fingers crossed.

Wild murmurs in the linoleum stirred your feet from the screen door, pulled away from
stale waiting rooms. Children breathing coughs into our home.
Around seven those anecdotes did not appear,
And Darling—your body missed the cue to barge through.

I barged one night, in my sleep. At the hallways entrance, you waved goodbye—
butI made my way back.
Dreams, Darling—Dreams
fruition fiercely moved from my bed to yours,
without ever waking your slumber,
Around two the paralysis ended
upside down beneath the extended night's white glare.

Cloudy and unsightly above my pupils.
I returned to the rabbit's shoulder,
Darling, my unconscious love, abandoned their posture Darling, the audacity.

Tomorrow's cigarette prematurely exhaled
conversations that were placeholders, a routine,
Yours, little more than an intellectual exercise—
A bumbling professor and their inquisitive pupil
approaching foreplay,
on my end of the porch.
willing to play the triangle,
Every Time
the wand hits, my bruising turns a little more blue.

To sit with you and him.
Darling—to make eye contact when he had the audacity, I made the tea.
But Darling, *please don't worry,*
I made tea for myself as well,

Darling, *my* nourishment comes from quenching *his* thirst.

Darling, I only joke, with bruises scribbled underneath,
inhaling glitter projected from the lava lamp's gaze.

Darling, more than a rupture in the veins rising from the stove.
It trickles below the burner to reach your toes
pressed against my soft cheek. She will crush my head
and I will not strike her heel.

Darling, ancestral bonds are vulnerable ones,
but soulmate ties are nerve racking when discernment
used to be so black and white.
Darling, we followed the feet in front of me
uncritically and with passive opulence.

Darling, I miss you, I cannot return to the porch, I am pinned down and chopped in half.

Emotional Embrace – Ashley Matarama (she/her)

1945 – DC Diamondopolous (she/her)

I first saw Teresa out my kitchen window back in 1928. Her father, a widower, had moved into our neighborhood. I was kneading dough when I looked up and watched the child glide her sled down a snowbank and slam into a tree. I ran across the street. "Are you hurt?"

She scowled. "Mind your own beeswax."

I ignored her sass and asked if she would like a nice piece of hot homemade bread. She rubbed her bump with a snow-crusted mitten and shook her head. Teresa repeated the stunt and sailed free all the way to the sidewalk. I clapped my doughy hands. The little one smiled. "Can my pop have one too?"

The next year the stock market crashed, and we plunged into the Depression.

I'd see Teresa walk home from school, alone, shoulders slumped, eyes downcast. We all wore threadbare clothes, but her charity hand-me-downs never fit her growing body.

One day, I invited her to see Shirley Temple in *Bright Eyes.* Coming out of the theatre, she reached for my hand, such sweetness in her grasp. From then on I became her cheerleader, my pompoms the crocheted scarves and sweaters I made for her.

From the end of the Depression to another War, changes occurred every minute—and right here, in Farmingdale, New York.

In the winter of '42, Teresa got a job at the Brooklyn Navy Yard. I'd be at my window at six o'clock making dinner as she arrived home in a car full of girls. She ran with newfound joy up the steps to the front door, turned, and waved first to her friends then to me. Her smile brought riches not even Rockefeller could buy.

Teresa had every other Sunday off and we'd have lunch on my back porch. "Oh Aunt Lena, I never knew working with my hands could be so much fun. There's a lot of us gals, cutting and soldering, doing everything the men did. But our paychecks are nothing compared to what they earned."

"Of course not. Men have families to care for." My comment hung in the air like a barrage balloon.

Why, I never questioned my pay working in the factory during the First World War. It would've been unpatriotic—but this, I kept to myself. Now we could vote. Women smoked. Teresa wore overalls at work—so much had changed.

On a spring day in '43, she told me about her promotion. "I work on submarines, welding." She put down her fork.

"What's wrong, dear?"

"They're cramped quarters. My boss rubs up against me. When I told him to stop, he put me out in the rain to weld, knowing I'd get electrical shocks."

"Can't you go to his boss?"

She shook her head. "It's always the girls' fault."

I worried that after the war, young women like Teresa, who built our ships, tanks and planes would question traditions. Men wouldn't stand for it. If I went to work, Roy would raise Cain, though he did let me sell war bonds.

In '44, Teresa made management, and our lovely Sunday lunchtimes came to an end. Her new boss, a decent man, depended on her. She worked twelve-hour days, seven days a week, and took care of her ailing father.

I helped out by sitting with Pop. One night when she returned late I expressed concern for her coming home alone in the dark.

She laughed. "With the boys gone, we girls can walk anywhere day or night and feel safe. Even Central Park."

Her breezy comment gave me chills. I saw thunderclouds on the horizon. "You respect our boys who are fighting for our freedom, don't you?"

"Oh Aunt Lena." She put her arm around my shoulder. "Of course, I do. But women are fighting for freedom too. Just not on battlefields."

The war in Europe ended May 8, 1945, but it dragged on in the Pacific.

Teresa's final promotion came in early June. She oversaw seventy-five women in the construction department. I couldn't have been prouder of her.

On August 15, the radio blared, "Official! Truman announces Japanese surrender."

"Aunt Lena, Uncle Roy!"

We all had tears in our eyes as I opened the door.

"I'm going to Times Square, then on to the shipyard. Can you look in on Pop?"

"Of course, dear." A car waited for her. The girls waved flags. I held up two fingers making a V for Victory. "Do tell me everything that happens."

Roy and I went back to the radio. We heard about the thousands of people who turned out in cities across America. I imagined the red, white and blue rippling and waving, confetti and ribbons, wet eyes and cheering—if only our beloved FDR had lived to see it.

That night we grew anxious as the hours passed and no word from Teresa.

The next morning I recall burning myself on the skillet. My mind filled with worry about our girl. Then from my kitchen window I saw her come out the front door. She wore slacks and a blouse and marched down the walkway to the car. Rigid—with dark smudges beneath her eyes.

I ran across the street. "What's the matter?"

"We wouldn't quit, so they fired us."

A girl in the car said, "With the boys coming home, we got canned."

"Of course. They'll need their jobs back."

Teresa glared at me. "My boss told me to get married and have babies."

"What did you expect?"

Teresa opened the car door. "I expected more from my country."

Back then I didn't understand the full impact of the war and what its aftermath meant to our daughters.

Now with Roy gone and Teresa out west, I think about those days and the car full of girls who worked at the Brooklyn Navy Yard. I know now as I watched them drive off to gather and speak up for their rights that what I saw was the future.

“Horses fuck inside me” – Zach Arnett (he/him)

We can’t name the horses as they do hurry
skurry. Nor their dry mouths and hair waxed
into the floor forever. We can’t name the sound
of twenty-eight gauge pins flailing or what that
costs in money. Heart of the ocean much?
We never caught the Reynauds above my
neck, so by apple picking I’m a crass and
perverted ghost. We can’t name the future
of balloon-supported lake walks, urinal handle
sweat, dog years of graffiti on the fucking Burger
Barn. We brought home the smell of propane
cans swaddled in the nest of a Nissan fork truck.
Are our smiles an expression of beet-
sweetened mustache? Keloid candy buttons
on your elbow, electric in the morning. Spines
pick a side to settle atop this refurbished
mammoth fabulously rich in nerve endings.
We can’t name the nuns at the chili bowl sale
scooping rice out of lemoned water.
We can’t taste red stacks of non-conforming
tags. Huff eighty grit down to the original wood.
We can’t name where it hurts when we look.

S'well – Zach Arnett (he/him)

You need marshmallow
to work as innards.
Family Dollar's out of innards.
You need red 40
to pass as real blood.
Family Dollar's out of real blood!
Staple me into this hospital bill that
says it's not a bill then empty your
your kid-head of mortal bondage—
The salt content of celery juice,
Schrader vs Presta valves,
caution tape wrapped upside down.
Yeah, and that app forecasts
the decaying fox back to life
refreshing choke cherries
in the first snow—yadda yadda...
Air escapes the Dyson Hand Blade
like fasolah, all smooshed together.
When I got sober I shoved my
heart on the AM bus to wilderness
camp somewhere in Utah.
She walked back out of the
mountains 12 pull-ups abler
flashing Too Small in my terrible master.
The thing is Addy's getting old
Time now fits in both hands.
What is ours here and what are just days.
Days, endless days of thin burritos—
Before, this flattering mo-cap suit
realized the green around us, now,
I couldn't feel further from my mother.

Alyssa? Alyssa. – Zach Arnett (he/him)

The PCH dissolves on my tongue
and makes this road trip taste short.

Honk if you'll grow different,
separate from all that is dear and appealing to you.

Really shitty 90's Mustangs. Randy Savage
hot dog skin. Hooves, assholes, and teeth.

My next tattoo connects the rash.
Your love makes a fist in me.

2013—year of flames pointing up. The Colts made
the Bud Light can. Cousins I'll just stop talking to.

I'll carry a pillowcase full of your dry shampoo
and deeply crave an end to fear.

My next tattoo writes, "Speak legibly into the grace of God."
As it escapes my head in steam.

Last Free-Standing Carousel – Zach Arnett (he/him)

Maybe the mayor's keen on coxswain polos, gauss checks,
the bottle redemption center, everything hard but never gives,
DUI cops, clean piss and placebo, the Trump metaphor,
big meat head surfers punching in watermelons, Deion's
40 time, the knife between his teeth, heel dumps
and otherwise the common folk. We clean the fridge
on Fridays in this office. We don't know Logansport
from Newport Outlet suite, but my mug says "Happy
to Serve You." I measure its roundness. The hole
shrinks as I watch. Mrs. Conliff finds little dead bird
heads from the mating peregrines atop the IMP annex.
It chugs a whisper reed of smoke to cough the Kokomo
out of me. Do you go to Logansport for the frisbee golf?
Well, do you go to Disney for the milk? No one answers.
Not Jefferson who found a swatch to match an irritation
on his hip. Not Dan, Local 4863, who slipped a camo cover
on his Wi-Fi'd couch. No one in the Festival Tour seat.
Not even the mayor. We just want our casts off before prom
if only to get the Hefty bags out of the shower. Our grenades?
A bunch of grapes. We want to hear our head flush through
our nose. This many whippet duds in the gulge? Of course,
they can't mix Jeff's shade. Of course, the couch stuck in recline.

IN THE DAYS OF OUR CHANGES – Margo Berdeshevsky (she/her)

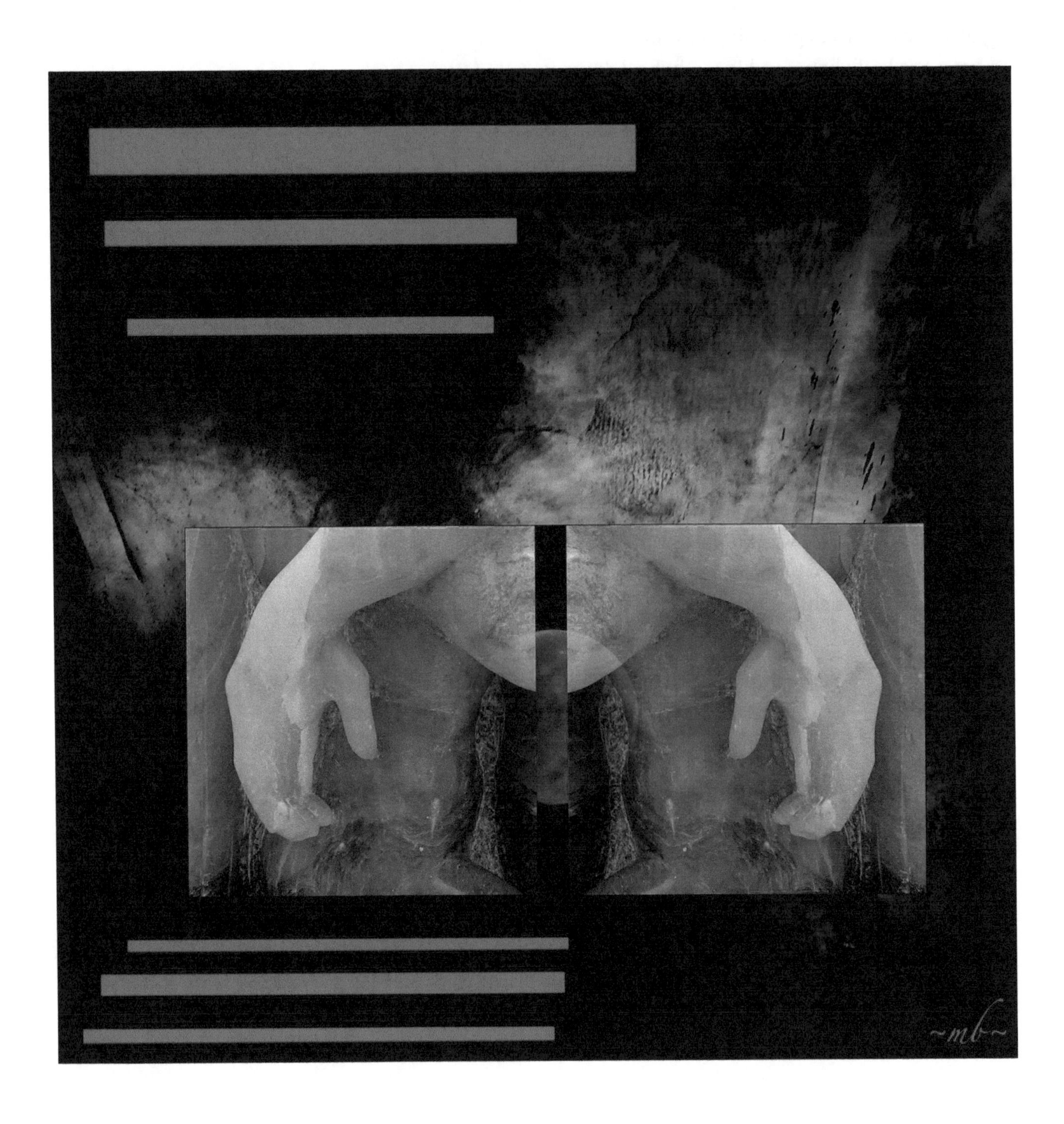

A WOLF MOON...AND THEN I HEARD FRENCH WOMEN SPEAK – **Margo Berdeshevsky** (she/her)

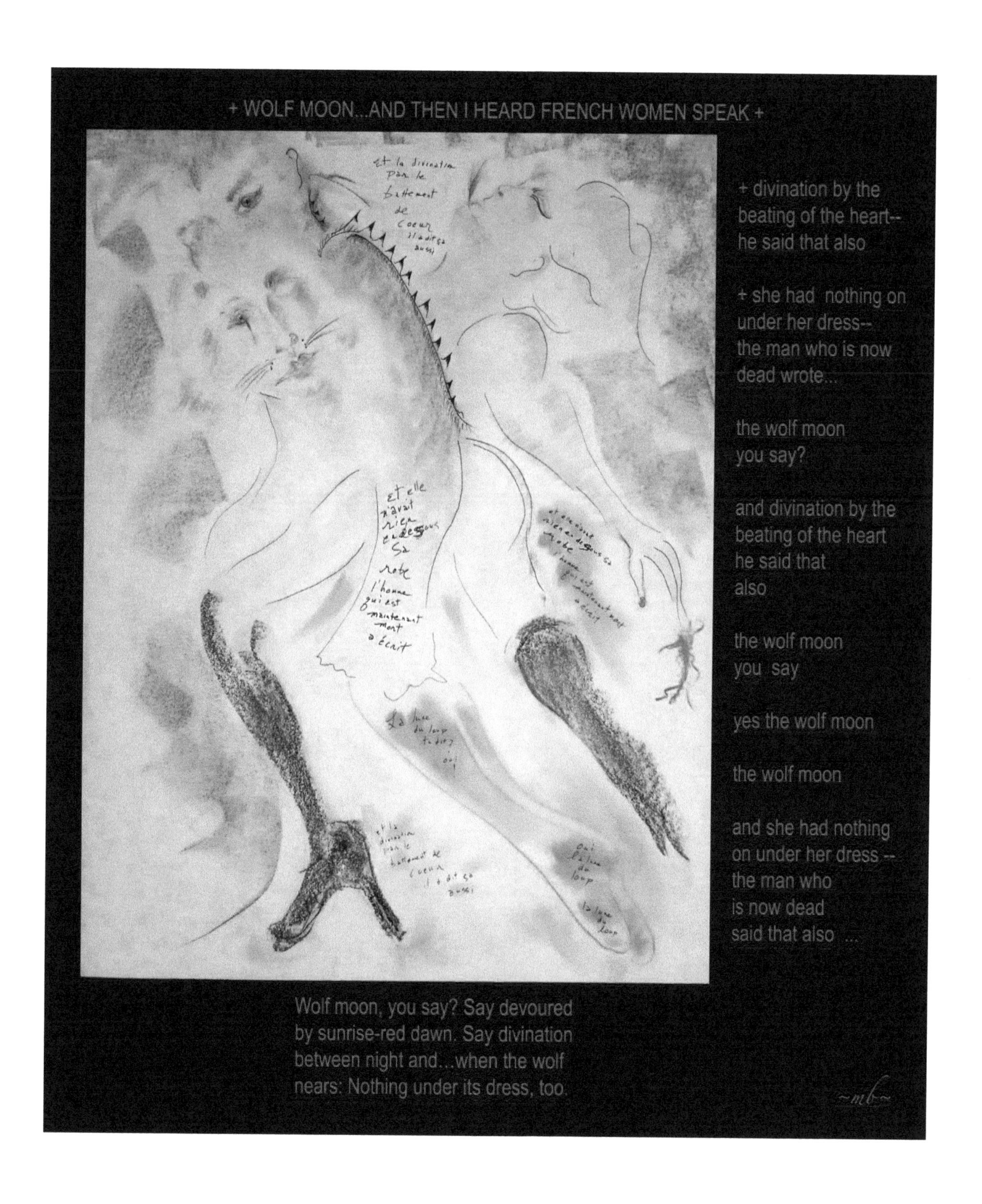

IN THE EMBRACE OF MY TIMES – **Margo Berdeshevsky** (she/her)

IN THE SHADOW OF BIRTH – Margo Berdeshevsky (she/her)

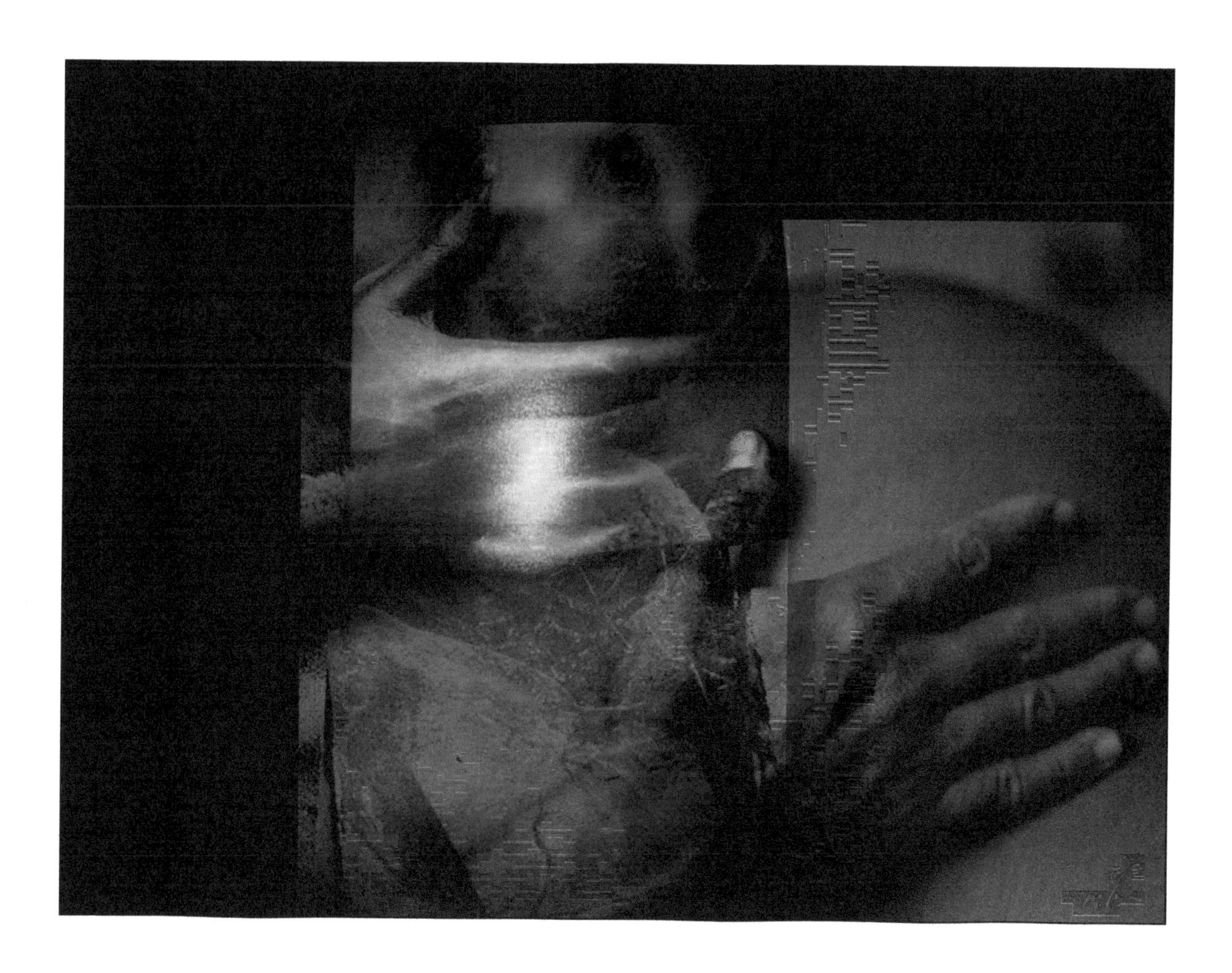

ON INTERNATIONAL WOMEN'S DAY – Margo Berdeshevsky (she/her)

Romeo and Juliet a Possibility – Rachael Ikins (she/her)

When you clean,
a bride into flames
you create room.
A lay-me-down love
you think you will never forget.

Beneath leaf mast,
a cup, sticky sweet liquid.
Lay me down, love,
measure your sweaty neck.

Brimming eyes, good girl,
what could-have-been, at twelve
warmth before the pyre,
this broiling maw of now.

Memories rake ragged nails
across the small of her back.
Someone's hand,
fingers braceleting wrists.
Such a shimmer
he'd pulled from his pockets

that Tuesday last July.
White shorts.
Her gown fluttering,
heat-crazed flame.

Elsewhere on the mountain
a flower, a vase.
Kali's terrifying indifference
rubs shoulders raw.

Her hand a shivering bird
married rearrangement,
blizzard swallows her.
Old sadnesses whisper.

Rubies as long as fingers.
The living, the snake sunning,
gagged her, his nakedness
backlit snow-spit.
Erase such shining wet,
buttocks frozen, his skin—

He can't feel
She can't feel
Lay-me-down, love,
Lay me down. We watch
helpers kill them.

When We Hang Colored Lights – Rachael Ikins (she/her)

Early darkness this time of year we become ghosts, impossible-to-see foot prints in the snow, you try to follow, tripping over each booted pockmark, sure you'll face-plant into the next lavender drift.

Blue bluff holds the imprint, a blurred face, a dent for a nose, blinded eyes see only ghosts. They know your name. Careful not to think about them too hard, do not meet their eyes, eye contact mesmerizes, it dissolves all the castles you built.

You know only their exquisite sting. You shiver as earth opens beneath you, your arms windmill, try to fly, but your dead feet are one with ice, and as spirit leaves body you dangle, wind rummages through your skull's drawer, calls you 1000 names. You struggle to remember who you are. You beg the words remain in place before you become a ghost, too.

Your immune system recognizes the intruder first, lassitude creeps, pouring fatigue that morphs cold into heat. You beg the words remain in place as the invader sucks your marrow. Chimeras skate across dunes/drifts, upended buckets of sand. Who knew the desert froze this hard? Wind scours blood with scaled fingers.

Moon stares then covers her face. Earth cocks her head to listen for your heart's percussion.

Look up. Clouds shine pewter, an occasional needlepoint star pricks a knot of blood, black in the night as the spirit leaves your body. Dawn shoulders night westward, a gray smolder reminiscent of thunder.

Light lifts morning's wall on its yellow back, with gold hands shoves overhead, day/night balanced. Before you become ghosts, in the timeless moment of 5 a.m. you want light. At 7:00 as lemon licks clouds' underbelly, you turn your face back toward death, not yet willing for so much revelation.

So Close: The Watcher – Rachael Ikins (she/her)

I was on the wall hunting flies in the sun
When the big black cars pulled up.
Men running with guns, doors slammed. Vibrations
traveled through
my feet. I slid into shadow.

I was on the garage wall the day the white van drove in.
Young man, scabbed and sweaty left a handprint just below
my perch. Garage door rumbled up. Voices raised. Shouting.
I caught a fat fly that
day. It never saw me.

I saw the blonde girl many times. She played with small boys in the backyard.
She never let them catch lizards in jars or step on ants, squatting with them,
three heads focussed on the way worker ants carry their eggs to safety after
rain floods their burrow.

Sometimes he hit her.
I saw the man who came home without her leave, my body still warmed
by sunlight-soaked stucco, awake. His movements those of a predator.

I see the television through their window, pictures of the blonde girl in
faraway deserts where other lizards live.
Maybe when he finished, squeezed
her neck so hard her feet didn't touch the ground,
maybe she fell off, he threw her off

into a wash below, limbs crooked as a tumbleweed.
Maybe some lizards sniffed
her, lay against her, absorbed her body's floating heat.
Maybe other lizards ate the flies
that landed in her tangled hair, mosquitoes that gathered
around puddled blood.

I follow the sun on the house walls,
day droops toward night.
There are cameras,
microphones, but nobody sees me
except an older woman
watching the news far away.

She cries for the broken girl who died in plain sight
while everybody watched.
Invisible, like a lizard blended into tree bark,
so many lost young women.
The words "Let it be."
inked on her arm.

Farts and other pleasurable hassles
– Liz Darrell (she/her)

Joys of Maintenance – Liz Darrell (she/her)

Venus Divine – Liz Darrell (she/her)

Pay it no mind – Liz Darrell (she/her)

Poem Not to Be Read at Your Church – Rye Owen (they/them)

—After Beth Anne Fennelly

You ask me for a poem for Christmas
in place of an art piece, that I might have made
in the past. For this night I've stared
at the glow of my computer screen at midnight
with the lights out. I've listened to the tick of heating
in a quiet house. Well, Mother, I would rather
deal with the silent disappointment of nothing
than write a poem for church. Let me find you
something else, a generic google poem. Don't
make me warn you of religion, how they see us
from the pulpit as malleable and worthless
from the dumb sheep that Jesus led
to the one-in-a-million little savior statue
holding his ripe, red heart in his hands.

Rye

Define Me – Rye Owen (they/them)

Morriah, noun

Pronunciation: mɔr raɪ yə
Origin: Parents
Etymology: Biblical Hebrew of the Old Testament, *Moriah*

1. God teaches
2. What a strange mission for a little child; what were they meant to teach, how not to be cruel to those who are different from white Christian
3. first tester child who only wanted to be loved fully for who they were

Usage: Archaic, 2001-2020
Often confused with: Mariah Carey

Rye, noun

Pronunciation: raɪ
Origin: name holder in college
Etymology: derivative of birth name

1. a type of grain used in cereal, bread, and other similar products
2. a thing; non-binary naming tradition like moss
3. freedom to hide; a slipup in front of those who I hide in the closet from shouldn't be considered anything but a new nickname
4. a person that is coming into their own and finding their footing despite the ground being oh so unsteady

Usage: Common, 2020 onwards
Often confused with: Ri, Ry, Rie

Emrys, noun

Pronunciation: ɛm rɪs
Origin: a mind fascinated with fantasy
Etymology: the druidic name of Merlin

1. Immortal
2. a want to be remembered as you are rather than as someone thinks you are; reality over fantasy
3. to be used in the fanfiction for the purpose of hearing a name without hearing it; a test of validity
4. It became too feminine feeling

Usage: In thought, June 2021-August 2022
Often confused with: Merlin, Ambrosius

Silas, noun

Pronunciation: saɪlæs
Origin: a mind that was trying to balance the beautiful with the meaning
Etymology: derivative of Sylvanus, a Roman god of the forest

1. a protector; of what, for me, the self
2. to be explicitly used when Sylvannus is the full first name, spelling pending as suggestion of friend says that the last four letters makes 'anus'
3. to be used in the fanfiction for the purpose of hearing a name without hearing it; a test of comfortability
4. a settling sound in the back of my stressed mind; may be sonorous soon

Usage: In thought, February 2022 onwards
Often confused with: Selwyn, Silvia

Home Sweet Home – Meghan King (she/her)

Home is a haven
A sanctuary, a child's safe place
Security
Upon divorce and when not in my father's care
This was lacking for most of my childhood
Stability was in the care of others
Stability due to lack of sobriety was a rarity
With my mother's struggle came a life not meant for a child
Home was filled with uncertainty
One child looking out for an even younger child
Ensuring my brother was sheltered from it
As much as a child of 8 could protect another

Blueprints – Meghan King (she/her)

Mi vida, Mi corazon
Cuidado, por favor
Please, take care of my heart
I tripped, fell in love
Defeated once to your hubris
Stumbling Down the Rabbit Hole
Depression in shadows
Searching for a beacon
I found courage
Created blueprints
Of self-love, respect
New, greater boundaries
Mi vida, Mi corazon
Cuidado, por favor
If you want the same, speak it plainly
If you want a shared life
Speak it true

wanting, wanton – Mikayla Elias (they/them)

there is no place among the clouds.
it is all passing farmland to the untrained eye,
one which fails to see
all the ways the grass glimmers blue and yellow.
I push back and recoil from touch
and am met with thorns below my ribcage,
in the fragile part of my center.
there was no snow in the wild Beyond.
there was only love, unreachable.
only time, impassable.
your name fires blue light into my pocket
and I obediently return, distant
with the fiction of adoration.
for you, I would purchase a thousand lamps,
huddle beneath for warmth, blinded,
and you would cut their cords to be
my only source of heat.
hot hands, hot breath, hot sex—
I could only find shelter in you.
wood wicks crackle and set off the fire alarms
but as long as I was yours,
we could burn alive.
there is no sun in the great Before.
we coast among condensed dew drops
and they muck up the way the stars
gaze back at us, envious of our youth.

daylily – Mikayla Elias (they/them)

"sacred" is to be godly
how is it that cloth,
spun cotton and polyester,
can be sacred indeed?
we imbue our own
holy spirit in the colors,
sun-bleached and downtrodden
meant to be cast
like a web between eaves
we kiss the tattered
edges and drape the
fabric like silk linens
on daybeds adorned in
daylilies, what a gift
it is to be crafted
sacred from filthy palms
and made whole

YOUR NAILS WILL TALK – Shrutidhora P Mohor (she/her)

My feet are like jellyfish, wobbly, squishy, boop-worthy.

Your legs are long and strong, muscular, and criss-crossed by lanes and creeks.

There are thorns on my roses. They prick my tender green skin and ask me to put on my trousers and sneakers and join the under-seventeen boys' rugby team. I wriggle in discomfort when I see the other boys, shorts-clad, their bony legs strutting across the field like those of an ostrich.

At night, I hide in darkness behind the door of the toilet. When I undress for the night, I cup the palms of my hands and hold them over my flat chest. When you arrive at the downtown inn, I invite you to trek up the hills. You smirk and check out. You'll like it, I cry out. Try the view from the top once. You shake your head. Nope, sissy, I have better journeys to undertake.

You are about to exit. You pause and add, plus, your nails look like the shit of a dead lizard. Cold, white, lifeless. They drive me away. You flash your teeth and walk away. Your long and strong legs look disappointed in me.

One day, I sit putting nail-polish on my lean fingernails.

I had been visiting the local parlour for some days before that. Your Nails Will Talk, reads its signboard. Excuse me, I had whispered from the entrance the first day. A bunch of chatty girls had not cared to hear me. I had moved up to the dressing counter, tiptoeing, not allowing my pencil heels to create a staccato. I had run my hands over manicure appliances and boxes of nail-art. They had seemed to be perfectly what I wanted. One of the staff had noticed me when she had turned back to pick her phone up.

"Son, you will have to take a package, pay for it, and then come for the service, understood?" A middle-aged woman had growled.

Then they had resumed chatting and laughing.

I had stood for some minutes and had gradually retreated out of the door.

Later that evening, I had done my school homework thoroughly, ensuring that all my sums would be correct and all my English grammar exercises perfect. When the grades had come two days later, I had carried my grade card to my dad's chamber. When he had patted me on my back while looking through his missed call lists, I had asked for some extra pocket money. "It's Laura's birthday next week."

He had shoved some notes into my hands and said, "Wish her on my behalf too and get her a good gift. Right, sweetie? Anything more?"

I had muttered a hazy no, nothing, thank you, sure, and left the office.

"You can do it yourself at home, son. Why visit the parlour? Boys don't come here." The middle-aged woman had whispered one day after I had been visiting them for some weeks.

Since then, I put my own nail-polish. Fluorescent green, febrile maroon, stars and mickey mouse faces as mini stickers on them.

I can see your legs approaching. I spread my fingers out and look coy. You are almost here. I decked up my nails for you, I move my lips even though my eyes are shut.

What's up, sissy? Been dressing up?

Before I can open my eyes and speak, I hear a purring voice from behind you, "Honey, see if you can fix the latch here. The door isn't shutting."

You turn back and disappear inside with your fiancée.

Atticus – Michael Putorti (he/him)

Angelique – Michael Putorti (he/him)

Piece – Sami Ridge (she/her)

And why
split the stem
 that
        makes you?
Because
 I can   make another.
Recreation without sincere   delineation.
[Just give it time]
Nevermind
        the work.
What does the stem say?
Sure, let's   no, not today   maybe if
hanging   ripped   a third too many.
Recycling itself into harried peonies.
stop.
But why-
Wholeness
makes our bread;
we know the story there
  something bred   solely
for breakage.
And that's it, that's-
Rise warm like women.
Be a flavor. Make an offer.
We were grains once
though some stood taller.
And you-

Yes. Of course,   always.

Mother – Sami Ridge (she/her)

And did her mucid baby feet
touch the moon
in its
holes? Or
did I own
anything?
You
who never knew
quite when to excrete
your centaur spirit,
but I'm sure if
I tried I could
remember myself
a heather
foal,
your lipstick
leaking ash into
my tummy
ventricular
samskara; those
heavenly bodies
cut
in cottoned coral
quadrilaterallly
at your breast, I
loved that shirt
in its lack
of here,
and I'd cease
before
I burned the hair
I trial every morning
to recreate.

But it's sordid
to think long
after
learning the ways
and the water leaving
how much
you had me drink, how
fine a filament
hung for years
the dendritic
stink of our bargain.
That shirt's somewhere
for purchase
and baby,
I'm no longer
a vacancy.

The Matriarch – Sami Ridge (she/her)

Procreative truths
plant their prisms
in a potted matrix; a
piece, see,
  for the opal
place
 that fixes me.
Grafting action
    as this choice
dictates creates the
soul and hide
life
more than
judicial resin
more than art
or pay or traditional
traction
at six for dinner,
sharp.
Chakral butter
permeates in every
singing limb I
train; in every
negation I have
killed. That
foliage, tender with
striation, with
finger-swirled pearls
of wild-berry, keeps
our fingers crossed and
our dirty knuckles
stroking the age from
our raw
jaws; more importantly
keeping our
corrugated truths
    so stellar.

I do,
surely
        want the
purchased entrapped
scorpions singing
in their shrapnels; I
want the liquid prowl
and feline play
swaying
the chutes at noon. Every room
rocks to sleep
    a thesis, the boas
in their sacred box and
the dogs in a stinking
heap. I'll bear down
in the deep
  shaping dense laundry
wrap myself
in hefty wool
and full, even flow, knowing
full that patriarchal plywood
keeps outside
with the wilderness that
loves Him. In that
moonlit hour, with
the run
of Nature's navel
thoughts arrive.

Aging Anthelion – Sami Ridge (she/her)

I scattered
at the apex
of the dream; that
white
crash of the
age
a bulb
in flash for
all us
dim pursuers.
My contents keep
their blessings, hot
a mess
of forfeit coaxed
to rose oil, soaked
with constant
contraction
of concept…
unfurled
peonies
pink navel
Maine coon
bore
no more in
subjugation
than an aeon
before Christ;
Textural in tandem
in the thrush thrash
of your briared lobe
thus far,
I find some luxury.
Until the close
of the air's
crocus clasp, I'll
ask for patience
of shades of minutes
for forest-fire focus
and the mien
of a girl
in gaining.

Sin – Sami Ridge (she/her)

Ink – Charles K. Carter (they/he)

The comforter yawns off his nude hip.
A yellow egg cracked open
gives birth to the point of a prism,
triangulated rainbow light shining
from the underside of a metallic grey UFO.
The lower rim of the spacecraft
is decorated in a string of small white lights.
This is the tattoo on his upper left glute.
His UFO is pristine and shapely
because he is always pristine and in-shape.

I am the opposite.
The sharp pointed stars that were inked
on my slimmer teenage hips
have rounded with the ebb and flow of age
as I overeat when feeling suicidal,
swelling up like a hot air balloon.
Sometimes I lose weight
when I get in the habit of angry jogging again,
but the pounds always find their way back,
stretching my constellations.

Lovework – Charles K. Carter (they/he)

To actively fix my relationship,
I agreed to marriage counseling.

Intimacy has always been an issue.
I want sex too much and he doesn't.

He wants to just hold each other
and make out and that gets me hard.

Our counselor asked us to set a recurring
one-hour timer for when we are together.

Every time the sixty-minute timer goes off,
we are required to kiss for sixty seconds.

No exceptions. No skips. No fucking. Just kissing.
So here we are stealing sweet kisses at rock concerts

and on backroads home from my grandmother's house
and in the confessional booth at his aunt's funeral.

Live Bait – Charles K. Carter (they/he)

I am a minnow,
snatched up by a firm human grip
— caught, bruised, and wriggling
in his calloused fingers.
He drives a hook through
the center of my body.

And then I am flying,
wind tickling my hurt.

I fall prey to a larger fish
and I think, *this is it;*
finally some peace
at the end of this pain.

I go down the narrow opening of the throat
but then I am yanked out,
past gill, scraping against sharp teeth.

And I am choking on human air again.

And then I am flying again.

And I am swallowed again.

And again and again and again
until my will to wiggle free turns still
on the water's surface.

phase – Julia Bortolussi (she/they)

i hope it's a phase you said it would be i hope it's a phase i hope it's a phase and i thought i wouldn't want it to i hope it's a phase i hope it's a phase but now i see the fog i hope it's a phase i hope it's a phase i hope it's a phase and hope it can pass and that i hope it's
a phase
my body never i hope it's a phase i hope it's a phase flips between realities again & i hope it's
i hope it's a phase i hope it's a phase i hope it's a phase i hope it's a phase i hope it's a phase i find
unreality in the uneven
and floods in the unfamiliar
phasing out is bliss flying from freedom is a bittersweet curse
don't let me be stuck i can't climb don't let me be stuck don't let me be stuck and i couldn't prepare for this don't let me be stuck don't let me be stuck the ground i once stood on is don't let me be stuck don't let me be stuck biting my ankles don't let me be stuck

i beg i plead i cry
until i hope that the monster in me washes away with
my inky dignity swirling the drain

save me from myself, you said you could
would you still, even when i proved to be the thing
you feared and rejected

*First published in *Messy Misfits Club Zine*

mask – Julia Bortolussi (she/they)

the colour pink,
forced in a barrage of misguided encouragements
soft rosy hues, too girl-ish
for the mould i was growing into
i could not wear it.
Defiant—you will not tell me
what i should abide by.

the low roof of a treehouse,
wood splintering into the shape of a roof
ducking, squinting against fresh sawdust
my lanky body crunched under the four by fours
          met with unsure stares, i am quick to leave to
          wither under the bright sun of the open sky.

a name that did not rhyme with my heart falling
from lips, meeting a wall
stinging like a cow's branding
permanently pressed under my skin.
this name is not my cross to bear,
i do not know it.

these, of all things, are not you
you are blooming flowers and an open fire
you rip the seams of a too-tight tee
and walk topless because you can

what is freedom?
you've tasted it all your life;
the swift minty kick
of not having to apologize

*First published in *en*gendered*

asexuality – Julia Bortolussi (she/they)

gave me a choice a reason to reconsider what i had been
told to reflect on who i've wanted to be and where it was
birthed: the most shallow parts of me yearned for others
but i did not know this was an option. cataclysmic moving parts brought
uncertainty and with it an unsatisfactory idea of
young adulthood as i climbed into the bed of sensuality. where am i?

to think i could be missing out and not know it at all; defeats
the purpose, yet i feel a pull of *lacking,*
tracing my steps back to the last time i felt anything and finding
nothing.

generations – Julia Bortolussi (she/they)

despite knowing better, i can't help but wonder
if us queers have generational trauma
that kick starts in our veins the moment we enter this fraught world and
intensifies as we learn our names,
tasting the discordance they are seen with

a queer, born with unnameable pain

you have been raised to know to hide before knowing what it means
yet your spirit jumps out at opportune moments

it's the way your young eyes saw a butch lesbian at the supermarket
with her lady on her arm
and you thought you'd seen true divinity
but were pushed into the next aisle before you could put a name to it

reader, this creation leapt into my head upon waking, before
a window was opened, a reason to cope:
happy transgender week of awareness
as if i have been spoken to in my dreams
by all the fallen queens and kings and
the voices long gone
living through fresh veins and a new generation

A rose by any other name - Elyssa Tappero (she/her)

What is in a name?
That which we call *Rosa*
by any other name would smell as sweet.
And yet we give each of a hundred species a name
and a name to each of a thousand cultivars.
Would you deny *Rosa persica* its singular title
or call *Rosa canina Rosa kordesii*?
Would you claim no difference
between the homes of *Rosa carolina* and *Rosa chinensis*
or the thorns of *Rosa acicularis* and *Rosa sericea*?
The humble rose is no less lovely with one name or another
yet we honor the beauty of difference
with the blessing of language.
If we can give each bud a family, genus, subgenus, and species
can we not respect the names with which
our fellow humans define themselves?
Are we not worthy of the same deference
as the smallest rose?

Tomboy - Elyssa Tappero (she/her)

I was a child who hated dresses yet wore my tangled hair so long it reached the base of my back. I performed in ballet recitals yet despised the makeup they required be plastered on my face. I loved glitter and stuffed animals and motorcycles and wooden swords. I was a princess, but I was one who could rescue herself.

I did not call myself a tomboy, though. The word fit awkwardly in my mouth even then, much like choir dresses and pink tights fit awkwardly on my chubby form. It's only in adulthood that I understand why I hesitated to claim the label: tomboy implied girl. To be a tomboy meant to be a girl who liked boy things, who was unlike 'normal' girls but who still, beneath the mud and the bruises, was a girl. And I was not a girl.

I was frozen pond water. Freshly mown grass. Coyotes howling in the night. I was wild blackberries and ripe apples and library books, wood smoke and Play-Doh and agates. I was thousands of memories and sensations squashed into the jelly bean-shaped body of a human child. They might have been consolidated under a given name and assigned gender but they never truly united into one concept. Yet what child worries about such things when they're tromping through wetlands or howling at the moon?

I've since shed the last of the dresses and most of my hair, and with them all the labels I once accepted (albeit with resignation) as my default. Replacing them with nothing has left me freer than since I was that blissfully unaware child. Besides, I am still her, still mushrooms and noisy crows and pressed pennies; we just understand us better now.

The flesh won't last forever - Elyssa Tappero (she/her)

At night I run my tongue over my teeth, the only bones I can touch, comforting myself that I am still a skeleton beneath all this soft meat. If I could I would carve away chunks of marbled fat and muscle to release the sexless, genderless framework within. How freeing to do away with all that weight! What a relief to discard all those features of the flesh which identify and define us! No breasts to enforce gender; no skin to determine privilege; no hair to cut, nails to trim, genitals to clothe, no daily burden of presentation at all. Just empty sockets and hard white lines and the eternal, effortless rictus grin. Pure calcium anonymity. I run my tongue over the sharp edges and smooth curves of my teeth and realize that although I do not love my body, perhaps I could love the skeleton buried inside. It did not choose the suffocating mountain of organs and expectations heaped upon it any more than I did. We are in this together, both physically and metaphorically—we should be allies. I run my tongue over my teeth and think, *Take care of me and I'll take care of you, bones. The flesh won't last forever, but you and I will.*

Self Portrait as Deer Lady at Rest – Anna Marie Ryan (she/her)

Sometimes I See Great Grandma's Face In The Night Skies Of Gallup – Anna Marie Ryan (she/her)

Plus-size mannequins in Victoria's Secret are someone's found family – Erin Clark (she/her)

Soft things, lady things, and silk separates.
Drawers more strap and gap than fabric.
The body spray I wouldn't allow myself
in adolescence. *Lovespell*: it belonged
to girly girls who'd wear tracksuits
with ass-stamped words. I was
mostly too tomboy for this
but always a little envious
of them, whose mothers
taught them makeup,
hair, nails, beyond
simple hygiene.
These days
she wears
mascara,
mother,
a middle-aged
glamour she permits
herself. Unlike then. I
am glad for her and hope
she chooses freely to augment
her beauty: not escaping age nor
prettifying for her second husband.
Meanwhile, I cannot bring myself to
do more than moisturize. Cannot care
enough to paint my skin, though I don't
begrudge those who do. Cannot begin to
know what to do with all this HAIR. There's
a billion dollar industry dedicated to denuding us
of all our furze, you know? But do I need to tame the
mane, lest I resemble Mary of Egypt, hirsute hermitess?

After Christmas sales: I strode through the door.
They'd brought in plus size mannequins: no
heads nor limbs, yet more real than any
ancient anorexic idols which repelled
even as they controlled me. It was
these, more than the religious
baggage, misused purity
put to shaming;
more than
mother's
busyness;
more than my
own baby butch
heart and hermeneutic
of suspicion. It was them,
those unattainable torsos that
I was meant to worship by imitation,
by displaying myself in strappy things.
It was them, it was those life sized fictions.
It was the ads what animated them: those Femme
Frankenstein's monster-dollars. It was them and how
I was told to look upon them. Look, and beyond myself.

Death tourism: Paris – Erin Clark (she/her)

—to Leroux, who has a lot to answer for

Since learning of
the Fantôme's manner

of escape
through the skull-

lined corridors,
I have wanted

to see them myself,
to fill my own

eye sockets with
the unlit space

of the quarry-
turned-ossuaire,

operatically,
a tenor at last.

i'm a 21st century stain (a ballad in 5 parts) – ellbeedee (they/them)

CW: gore

I.
there's so much meaning here
between floorboards and music scores
the peacefulness rots my soul to the bone
and i'm a walking gramophone
knowing i can only sing
when i'm alone
so tear my lungs to bits
and hide them there, where silence sits
out of the way of everyday drolls
because i need this space to flow
mold me;

II.
i've been screaming since womb's release
and if you think i'll ever keep the peace,
you're wrong; i long to burn you
in between my teeth, like old strings,
i know i cannot touch you, nor
will you ever be taught to see
people like me
are meant to be, so
unfold me;

III.
god, if you're up there, hear my gruesome prayer, tear down the chords that strung us up tight
took away these rights, unite the sight
behind these eyes before i'm blind again,
don't tell me that the lives of men still matter
because i am not a man,
thrice been, now never am
you see, i'm a grotesque:
undress these guts
and i'll bleed
behold me;

IV.

it's hard to believe there's something more once my foot's out the door and
you're running from prison
once you've chopped off our heads let the windpipes glisten
let me speak through my wheezes if it pleases you, sir
withhold me;

V.

so here i am, alone again
the only way to hear the pen as it strikes strikes strikes the page
breaks breaks breaks the cage
inky gore, caress these days
'cause they're sinking through
the languished haze
of all these old how-do-you-dos because
you can't
control me.

*Previously published in *all of the animals*

come the light – ellbeedee (they/them)

they all left at the same time
saying goodnight in that lifeless tone because
they knew we'd see each other again in the morning, anyways.

as i closed a few windows to keep out the draft
i knew i could not forget what they'd said to me and how lost they all were and how i
wanted nothing more than to. . . .

i dreamed of a world where we could talk forever tell all of our stories and whisper every single secret
the trees want to listen and they've been asking for weeks about that time when you were seven and
you found a tiny robin lying beneath its mother's nest and you nursed it back to health, but you
wouldn't dare tell your mom,
because she'd have left the little thing to

die

you still can't forget the day you took its broken body between your fingerprints,
it was the first time you were truly *there*.

(i want to hold you like the robin;
i want to be *there*, too.)

sometimes i stare out the window
because it's the only thing i can do to help you;
i wish i could be more useful, but all i really am
is some proteins and membranes that
can listen when you need eardrums to beat on,
even if all i can do is pound back too,
at least there's some freedom to our thunderstorm because no matter how
cacophonous your
quicksilver teardrops are when they hit my hands, i'll still hold onto them

forever.

reread – ellbeedee (they/them)

i'm cracking open my head like an egg with an embryo inside, not unlike a mirror, but one i've broken (unintentionally or not) before grabbing another to add to the bowl

it's a crisp sensation
of disillusionment in reverse
looking back on my own tapestry, and wondering "how did i get here, and why was this map so wrong?" i hang it up beside old insecurities, roll the tanned flesh between my fingers, the smell of life long passed

i'm left with a feeling of emptiness but not in the gutted sense, no,
there's plenty here, but who was i? i've never met someone so unlike myself;
i'm breathing in familiar spores
of growth i cannot fathom,
and this cracked parchment shows paths i don't remember taking.

ABOUT THE CONTRIBUTORS

- Alex Carrigan (he/him) is a Pushcart-nominated editor, poet, and critic. He is the author of *Now Let's Get Brunch: A Collection of RuPaul's Drag Race Twitter Poetry* (Querencia Press, 2023) and *May All Our Pain Be Champagne: A Collection of Real Housewives Twitter Poetry* (Alien Buddha Press, 2022). He lives in Alexandria, Virginia. For more information, visit carriganak.wordpress.com or follow him on Twitter @carriganak.

- Andrew Michael Joseph (he/him/his) is a queer, Asian-American artist from Albuquerque, New Mexico, whose creative practice centers around an exploration of the intersections of identity, and how that impacts the way a human body is perceived by society, intimate partners, friends, and family. He is inspired by his own experiences as a queer person of color and is motivated by a desire to explore and understand the way his identity has influenced how he navigates the world. He seeks to create work which challenges contemporary societal expectations as well as normalize the queer experience and find kinship and commonality at the intersections of different identities.

- Ambyunderock (they/them) is someone who enjoys whimsical and fantastical art. They like to draw characters and add lots of strong colors to inspire persons to think differently of what they once saw as singular. Instagram @Ambyunderock

- Anna Kohlweis (she/they) is an Austrian interdisciplinary artist working in writing, painting, music, sculpture, and film. Anna's poetry often lives in all disciplines simultaneously, changing shape and mediums throughout its life cycle.

- Anna Laura Falvey (she/her) is a Brooklyn-based poet and theater artist. She is a graduate of Bard College where she received degrees in Classics and Written Arts with specialization in ancient poetry and tragedy. Anna Laura served as a 2022-'23 ArtistYear Senior Fellow and resident teaching artist, teaching poetry in Queens, NY. Her written work is forthcoming with *Glint Literary Journal, Bloodletter Magazine*, and has appeared in *Evoke Magazine, Club Plum, Caustic Frolic, Ouch! Collective,* multiple issues of *Deep Overstock, Icarus Magazine,* and has been featured on the *Deep Overstock* podcast.

- Anna Marie Ryan (she/her) is visual artist and farmer who's family roots twine across the southeastern woodlands, into the corn belt Midwest, and through the southwestern desert; she is now grateful to call the unique land where the Rockies meet the Plains "home". Her paintings—done on scraps scavenged from her father's woodshop—explore identity in terms of the relationships between humans and the natural world, and the role (his)stories play in shaping our selfs!

- Anushka is a 21 year old writer based in India. She is a graduate in Psychology and wishes to be a Clinical Psychologist one day. Her work has previously appeared in Indian Periodical, Sunday Mornings At The River, and Sour Cherry Mag. One of her long term goals is to become a published author. Find her on Instagram @anushkkag

- Ashley Matarama (she/her) has a BFA in Animation and Illustration. She uses her creativity to communicate with the audience through visual storytelling.

- Bianca Alyssa Pérez was born and raised in Mission, Texas—a small southern town bordering Mexico. She holds her MFA in Poetry from Texas State University, where she also teaches. She is the 2022-2023 Clark House Writer-In-Residence. Her chapbook, *Gemini Gospel*, won *Host Publications'* Spring 2023 Chapbook Prize Contest. You can find her writing in *Magma Poetry UK, ReclamationATX,* Psst! Press' *The Sappho Diaries, East French Press, The New York Quarterly, Re-side Magazine, The Ice Colony Anthology* and *The Porter House Review*. She is also the co-host of the horror podcast, *Basement Girls*.

- Caspian is a writer, artist and professional tchotchke fanatic. Currently he's trying to figure out if you can paper mache a corset out of Pokémon cards.

- Charles K. Carter (they/he) is a queer poet who currently lives in Oregon. They are the author of several books, including *Read My Lips* (David Robert Books) and *Artificial Sweetness* (Finishing Line Press). He is also the creator and host of the video podcast series #SundaySweetChats. They can be found on Instagram and Twitter @CKCpoetry.

- Charlie J. Stephens is a queer, non-binary writer and the owner of Sea Wolf Books & Community Writing Center in Port Orford on the southern Oregon coast. Charlie's debut novel, "A Wounded Deer Leaps Highest" will be published by Torrey House Press May 2024. Charlie's short fiction has appeared in Electric Literature, Best Small Fictions, New World Writing, Original Plumbing, Feminist Press, and elsewhere. More at charliejstephenswriting.com and on Instagram @charliejstephenswriting.

- Cheryl Tan (she/her) is a Singaporean of Chinese and Indian descent. She has been published in Amber: The Teenage Chapbook, Ice Lolly Review, Cathartic Youth Literary Magazine, and *Eye on the World*, an anthology by the Creative Arts Programme, Singapore. In her free time, she writes poems and social commentaries by the sea, and hopes to write a book someday.

- Christina Lynn Lambert writes steamy paranormal romance novels as well as poetry. Her poems are about fighting for change, the beauty of nature, and trying to find the good moments in life. She lives in beautiful Virginia with her family.

- DC Diamondopolous is an award-winning short story, and flash fiction writer with hundreds of stories published internationally in print and online magazines, literary journals, and anthologies. DC's stories have appeared in: *Progenitor, 34th Parallel, So It Goes: The Literary Journal of the Kurt Vonnegut Museum and Library, Lunch Ticket,* and others. DC's recently released collection *Captured Up Close (20th Century Short-Short Stories)* has two Pushcart Prize nominated stories and one nominated for Best of the Net Anthology. Her first collection of stories was *Stepping Up*. She lives on the California coast with her wife and animals. dcdiamondopolous.com

- If you see a woman in Doc Martens drooling over a 1964 Chevy Impala like it's candy, it's probably Elaina. Her first two books are *Italian Bones in the Snow* and *Black Licorice.* Elaina's poems and prose have been published in various mags and journals. She lives on the Jersey Shore with her husband and daughters. Her essay "I Said it Out Loud" was a 2021 finalist in the *Anne Dillard* CNF contest

- ellbeedee (they/them) is a queer poet & witch. They make work inspired by their dreams, their magic, and the way they navigate the world. As a nonbinary & mentally ill person, their creations reflect their experiences as someone who doesn't fit into any distinct category of identity or medium. They live with their fiancé and have been focusing on book & textile arts alongside their writing endeavors.

- Elyssa Tappero (she/her) is radically queer, vocally pagan, and writes a lot of weird shit she hopes will leave you feeling vaguely disturbed. She enjoys alliteration, run-on sentences, killing characters, and making obscure references to historical events. You can find her work at onlyfragments.com and on Twitter at @OnlyFragments.

- Emily Perkovich is from the Chicago-land area. She is the Editor in Chief of Querencia Press and on the Women in Leadership Advisory Board with Valparaiso University. Her work strives to erase the stigma surrounding trauma victims and their responses. She is a Best of the Net nominee and a SAFTA scholarship recipient. She is previously published with Harness Magazine, Rogue Agent, Coffin Bell Journal, and Awakenings among others. She is the author of the poetry collections Godshots Wanted: Apply Within (Sunday Mornings at the River), The Number 12 Looks Just Like You (Finishing Line Press), & baby, sweetheart, honey (Alien Buddha Press) as well as the novella Swallow. You can find more of her work on IG @undermeyou

- Erin Clark (she/her) is a queer American writer and priest living in London, England. Her work has been published in the New Critique, the Oxonian Review, Geez, the Hour, About Place, The Primer, The Crank, Pilcrow & Dagger, and elsewhere. She is the author of the poetry pamphlet *Whom Sea Left Behind* (poetry pamphlet, 2023, Alien Buddha) the nonfiction *Sacred Pavement* (2021) and a coauthor of *The Book of Queer Prophets* (2020). Find her online at emclark.co or on Twitter @e_m_clark.

- Francesca Kritikos (@fmkrit) is the editor in chief of the journal and publisher SARKA. Her first full-length poetry collection, *Exercise in Desire*, was published by Vegetarian Alcoholic Press in 2022 and was selected as one of Bookshop.org's Staff Picks. Her poetry has been published recently by Hot Pink Mag, ITERANT, The Quarterless Review, Hobart, and Wonder. Links to her published works can be found at bio.site/fmkrit.

- Helen Coats (she/they) has a B.A. in creative and professional writing from Purdue University. They spend most of their time as a bookseller specializing in children's literature and the rest of the time onstage (as often as possible, anyway). Her work has been featured in bioStories, Gingerbread House, Toasted Cheese, and the Bell Tower.

- Irina Tall (Novikova) is an artist, graphic artist, illustrator. She graduated from the State Academy of Slavic Cultures with a degree in art, and also has a bachelor's degree in design. The first personal exhibition "My soul is like a wild hawk" (2002) was held in the museum of Maxim Bagdanovich. In her works, she raises themes of ecology, in 2005 she devoted a series of works to the Chernobyl disaster, draws on anti-war topics. The first big series she drew was The Red Book, dedicated to rare and endangered species of animals and birds. Writes fairy tales and poems, illustrates short stories. She draws various fantastic creatures: unicorns, animals with human faces, she especially likes the image of a man - a bird - Siren. In 2020, she took part in Poznań Art Week. Her work has been published in magazines: Gupsophila, Harpy Hybrid Review, Little Literary Living Room and others. In 2022, her short story was included in the collection "The 50 Best Short Stories", and her poem was published in the collection of poetry "The wonders of winter".

- j.g. bova (he/they) is a writer and senior student studying English (Creative Writing) at Salem State University, class of 2023. He was a founding leader of the SSU Writers' Group. Joseph received the SSU Creativity Award in Creative Writing in 2022 and the SSU Presidential Arts Scholarship. He has published several creative pieces in Salem State's *Red Skies Magazine* and served as the Managing Editor. They are currently finishing up their honors thesis project: an original fantasy audio drama called *Tales of Eilu* (advised by Professor Tanya Rodrigue). They have worked with the SSU Writing Center on several occasions as a tutor and course-embedded tutor. j. g. bova is also the Marketing Intern for MassPoetry, a nonprofit that works to bring poetry-related programming across Massachusetts. He is an inductee of both Sigma Tau Delta English Honor Society and Phi Kappa Phi Honor Society.

- Jai is an aspiring author who occasionally dabbles in poetry. They enjoy reading, writing, playing basketball, and learning about space. They've identified as queer since 2020 and are looking to write more stories about people like them. Put the content you want to see out into the world, right?

- Jake Price is a sophomore student at Susquehanna University pursuing a degree in creative writing. He spends most of his time reading his work to his cat, Raven, who has yet to give him any feedback. He was born in Texas and currently resides in Pennsylvania. Writing has been a passion of his for as long as he can remember, and he hopes to make it into his career one day. Jake has an Instagram account where he posts his poetry, @nolenprice, that has amassed over 3100 followers as of writing this. His poetry has been published in *Rivercraft Magazine*, *Poet Lore Magazine*, and *Cream Scene Carnival*.

- johanna monson geerts is a maker, writer, and explorer currently wandering the united states. she believes in the power of quiet art and ordinary stories.

- Joseph Soares is a writer from Ottawa, Ontario. He writes poetry, short stories, and creative nonfiction, often revolving around the themes of transness, madness, and addiction. His microchap Life Again can be found at *Kith Books*.

- Julia Bortolussi is a graduate of the Creative Writing & Publishing program at Sheridan College. She is the Assistant Poetry Editor for Augur Magazine, a Poetry Reader for diet milk magazine, and was the founding Head of Design for IntroSPECtion. You can find more of her work in Serendipity NewsMag, All My Relations, en*gendered, Snowflake Magazine, and more.

- Kaylee Hernandez, (she/they) is a working artist and recent graduate of the University of Texas Rio Grande Valley with a Master's Degree in Studio Art. As a queer artist working on the border of Mexico and the United States, she believes her unique perspective can help change the world! She hopes, anyway. In her spare time when she isn't feeding stray cats, she runs a small business making and selling vinyl stickers. https://www.kayleescameos.com/

- Kristin Lueke (she/her) is a Virgo, chingona, and author of the chapbook (in)different math (Dancing Girl Press). Her poems have appeared in the Acentos Review, HAD, Hooligan, the Santa Fe Reporter, Blue River Review, and elsewhere. She studied English at Princeton University and received an MA in Humanities and Creative Writing from the University of Chicago.

- Kristina Percy (she/her) lives on Vancouver Island, Canada in the traditional territories of the Ligwiłda'xw people. Neither of her degrees have anything to do with creative writing. Her work has been published extensively in her Gmail drafts folder

- László Aranyi (Frater Azmon) poet, anarchist, occultist from Hungary. Known spiritualist mediums, art and explores the relationship between magic.

- Liz Darrell is a queer multidisciplinary artist born and based in New York City. She was exposed to an absurd array of dramatic and visual arts growing up, perhaps triggering her perception of the world in expressive rather than logical ways. She relishes in the strangeness of being alive these days. There's a lot to think about, there's a lot to feel about, but there's even more to do. With her work, she aims to provoke something, anything. Be it internal or external; a thought or actions.

- Lydia Fern is a queer nonbinary trans woman, 25 years old, and a Taurus Rising. She is a white settler living on occupied ancestral and current Wintu homeland, colonially known as Redding, California. She likes plants, bugs, and systems, she is fascinated with tarot and astrology, and she likes to help people remember to be alive!

- Maegen McAuliffe O'Leary is a poet and mother from the Pacific Northwest. Her work focuses on the intersection of feminism, matrimony, motherhood, magic, and the human body and its place in nature. Her poems were most recently featured in publications from *Querencia Press, Quail Bell Magazine*, and *Nymeria Publishing*. Her debut chapbook, Bodies to Bury the Hunger, is available from *Bottlecap Press*.

- Mailene (She/They) is a 19-year-old queer person of color who was born and raised in Austin, Texas. She is currently pursuing her education at Texas State University. Mailene is an emerging poet, who finds solace in poetry and uses it as a medium to express her emotions. Her unique perspective and voice make her work both moving and thought-provoking. In her free time, Mailene can be found writing, reading, and advocating for social justice causes.

- MARGO BERDESHEVSKY, born in NYC, lives in Paris. Her newest book, "Kneel Said the Night (a hybrid book in half-notes)" is from Sundress Publications. Other books: "Before the Drought," /Glass Lyre Press, (finalist for National Poetry Series,) "It is Still Beautiful to Hear the Heart Beat" /forthcoming from Salmon Poetry; "Between Soul & Stone" and "But a Passage in Wilderness" /Sheep Meadow Press, "Beautiful Soon Enough," (recipient of 1st Ronald Sukenick Innovative Fiction Award for FC2 (U of Alabama Press). Recipient of grand prize for the Thomas Merton Poetry of the Sacred Award, the Robert H. Winner Award from the Poetry Society of America, her works appear in Poetry International, New Letters, The Night Heron Barks, Kenyon Review,

Plume, Scoundrel Time, The Collagist, Tupelo Quarterly, Gulf Coast, Southern Humanities Review, Harbor Review, Pleiades, Prairie Schooner, The American Journal of Poetry, Jacar—One, Mānoa, Pirene's Fountain, Big Other, Dark Matter: Women Witnessing, Bracken, and more. In Europe her works have been seen in The Poetry Review, PN Review, The Wolf, Europe, Siècle 21, Confluences Poétiques, Recours au Poème, Levure Littéraire, Under the Radar. Her "Letters from Paris" have appeared for many years in Poetry International online, for example: https://www.poetryinternationalonline.com/letter-from-paris-in-march-2019-from-margo-berdeshevsky/ . Find her reading from her books in London, Paris, New York City, Los Angeles, literary festivals, or somewhere new in the world. For more info, her website is: http://margoberdeshevsky.com

- Marissa Wolfe (she/her) is a poet and writer of fiction and creative non-fiction based in the foothills of South Carolina. When she is not tending to her garden, she is nursing a cyclical pile of unread books. You can find more of her writing on TheProse.com under her username, TheWolfeDen.

- Marsha Meyers (any pronouns with intention) is a 23 year old artist from southern California concerned with a variety of writing genres and visual mediums. Marsha plays with words and paints, nature and mysticism; especially when the elements coalesce unexpectedly. Trained in anthropological methodology, they love to infuse new perspectives into age old art forms. Their lifeforce is found in transforming late night insomnia journal entries and early morning rituals into semi-coherent language, infusing new epiphanies and persistent struggles into all their creative endeavors, and giggling with comrades over shared meals. To find more of Marsha's poetry and political commentary checkout their medium blog @comradesocial or their Instagram @marshameyerss.

- Megan Hatch (she/her) is a queer, multidisciplinary artist living in Portland, OR. After receiving a BA in studio art from Carleton College, she has spent many years creating work, teaching art in communal spaces, and curating exhibitions in often nontraditional environments. Her experiences of growing up rural, working class, and queer created a deep desire to make the arts accessible to a broader range of folks than typically find themselves, or at least comfortably so, in mainstream spaces. You can find her work at www.meganhatch.com.

- Meghan King is a Jersey born and raised writer. Meghan's most recent work is in Not Ghosts, But Spirits Vol I and Winter Anthology 2023 by Querencia Press. Her poem *Sovereign Hope* was featured in NJ Bards Poetry Review 2022 by Local Gems Press. She writes poetry and nonfiction on the resilience of the human spirit. Wanderlust runs through her veins. Coffee an elixir, laughter medicine, strength in her roots. She holds to the belief in being able to change the tide.

- Michael Putorti (He/Him/His) graduated from Slippery Rock University of Pennsylvania with a Bachelor of Fine Arts Degree. During his undergraduate career, his concentration was in printmaking, specifically linocuts. A lot of his work takes on a socio-cultural aspect. His subject matter consists of topics he feels are not discussed enough and wants his art to not only bring those issues to people's attention but also educate them on the issues that we face today. He has been in multiple online art exhibitions as well as been featured in physical galleries including "engendering Change" at the Cloyde Snook Gallery in Adams State University in Colorado, which focused on LGBTQ art.

- Mikayla Elias is a queer author from Nashville, Tennessee. Since turning from the world of audio engineering to the world of literature, they have published the poetry collection *Bending Toward the Light* and have been featured in samfiftyfour, Ouch! Collective, Pile Press, and Bullshit Lit.

- Mimi Flood (she/her) is the author of *Provocative is a Girls Name* (Querencia Press), *Slut Pop* (Dark Thirty Poetry Publishing), *and Baby Blue* (Bottlecap Press). She has been published in Dark Thirty Poetry Publishing, Querencia Press, The Graveyard Zine, Scar Tissue Magazine, Published With Papers, and Gypsophila. You can find her on Instagram @Marigold_Jesus.

- Pink Zombie Rose is made up of the talents Dia VanGunten and Beppi. Follow the story on IG @pinkzombierose — Beppi is currently finishing up The Hanged Man. Luckily for her, it doesn't seem to be her card—upright or reversed. She would love to say her card would be the one from the Charlie's Angels trading cards where Jill & Kelly look bad ass, caption "Ready for Danger!", but spending her life making art hasn't lead to a lot of danger. Although Beppi has found plenty of intrigue &, dare say, danger in the comics she illustrates. These stories are full of bad ass chicks, conspiracies, "zombies", magic, inclement weather, bullies, Joan Crawford, & much more. So get ready for danger! To see Beppi's work on IG @beppiisbert or www.circleofevil.com (her site is still in progress) & — Dia, the hanged man, card itself: strung up, all blood rushing to her head, as she edits Major Arcana, a fully illustrated collection of 22 Pink Zombie Rose stories. *To be released by Q, graphic imprint of Querencia Press*

- R S Kendle (she/they) is a poet from the north-east of Scotland. She holds a BA Honours in English Literature and Politics from the University Of Strathclyde. Her work has been published in several publications, including Feminist Space Camp, Free Verse Revolution, and The Survivor Zine. Her Instagram handle is @rskendle

- Raegen Pietrucha writes, edits, and consults creatively and professionally. Her debut full-length poetry collection, *Head of a Gorgon*, won a 2023 Human Relations Indie Book Award; her debut poetry chapbook, *An Animal I Can't Name*, won the 2015 Two of Cups Press competition; and she has a memoir in progress. She received her MFA from Bowling Green State University, where she was an assistant editor for *Mid-American Review*. Her writing has been published in *Cimarron Review*, *Puerto del Sol*, and other journals. Her photography has been published in *Rivanna Review*, *Seaside Gothic*, and other outlets. Connect with her at raegenmp.wordpress.com, on Twitter @freeradicalrp, and on Instagram @raegenmp.

- Rachael Ikins is a 2016/18 Pushcart, 2013/18 CNY Book Award, 2018 Independent Book Award winner, & 2019 Vinnie Ream & Faulkner poetry finalist, 2021 Best of the Net nominee, and author/illustrator of nine books in multiple genres. Her writing and artwork have appeared in journals worldwide from India, UK, Japan, Canada, and US.

- Rachel Coyne is a woman writer and painter from Lindstrom, MN

- Currently attending university at Salem State University, Rye Owen is a writer who follows their passions into realms of LGBTQ and fantasy themes, in poetry and prose.

- S. Kavi is a South Indian American poet, writer, and artist from Texas. Her work explores her cultural experiences, nostalgia, and healing. She was a finalist for Best of the Net 2023 and her work appears in antonym, Rhodora, The Indian Feminist Review, and elsewhere.

- Sadee Bee (she/they) is a queer artist and writer inspired by magic, strange dreams, and creepy vibes. Sadee is the Visual Arts Editor for Sage Cigarettes Magazine and the author of Pupa: Growth & Metamorphosis (Alien Buddha Press) and Magic Lives In Girls (kith books). Her visual artwork has also been exhibited by Influx Gallery. Sadee can be found on Twitter @SadeeBee, on Instagram @sadee__bee, and on the web at linktr.ee/SadeeBee.

- Samar Jade works in different artistic mediums to express themselves. They are passionate about fostering community and helping others to embrace their fullness. In addition to the creative arts they are a scholar working towards a PhD in ethnomusicology. Their research interests include Afrofuturism, Queer voices in music, Black Liberation and Sonic Geographies.

- Sami Ridge is a multi-disciplinary artist living in Seattle. She currently splits her time between professional art modeling and a wide array of projects, including a forthcoming E.P., a screenplay adaptation, poetry manuscript, multi-media art pieces, and several short story/novel ideas. Her progress can be watched from her Instagram, @samiridgethewriter.

- Shannon Clem (she/they) is a queer, neurodivergent, chronically ill spirit residing with their offspring in California. They have work published or forthcoming in *The Hunger, Anti-Heroin Chic, Bullshit Lit, Versification Zine, warning lines, MIDLVLMAG, Rat's Ass Review, Our Own Coordinates: Poems About Dementia* (Sídhe Press, 2023), & elsewhere. www.shannontantrum.com

- Shrutidhora P Mohor (born 1979) is an author from India writing literary fiction. She has been listed in several international writing competitions like Bristol Short Story Prize, the Bath Flash Fiction Award, the George Floyd Short Story Competition, Strands International Flash Fiction Competition, the Retreat West monthly micro, the Retreat West quarterly themed competition, Reflex Fiction, Flash 500, quarter 4 2022, the Retreat West quarterly unthemed competition. Her writings have been published by oranges journal, Fiery Scribe Review Magazine, National Flash Fiction Day Flash Flood, Ayaskala, Friday Flash Fiction, Courageous Creatives anthology, Spiritus Mundi Review, Contemporary Jo, Erato Magazine, Worm Moon Archive, Flash Fiction Magazine, Vestal Review issue; (nominated for this flash fiction piece to Best Micro fictions 2023), The Violet Hour Magazine), The Lovers Literary Journal (forthcoming), Bullshit Lit (forthcoming). Mohor (she/ her) is the pen name for Prothoma Rai Chaudhuri, MA Ph D, Faculty, Department of Political Science, St Xavier's College, Calcutta, India. Her Twitter handle is @ShrutidhoraPM and her Instagram username is @shrutidhorap

- Subhaga Crystal Bacon (she/they) is a Queer poet living in rural Washington on unceded Methow land. She is the author of four collections of poetry including *Surrender of Water in Hidden Places*, Red Flag Poetry published in April, and *Transitory*, forthcoming in the fall of 2023 from BOA Editions.

- Syd M is an non-binary POC Arab American poet that loves coffee and tea. Their work has been published by Querencia Press, Suspension Literary Magazine, Pile Press and Iceblink Lit.

- Veronica Szymankiewicz is a published poet from Miami, Florida. Her poetry varies quite a bit in genre and themes and is inspired directly from her own personal experiences, thoughts, and feelings. A lifelong writer and lover of words, she considers poetry to be a cathartic outlet. Veronica writes as a way to heal herself, with hopes that her words will resonate with others, healing them along the way as well.

- Vita Lerman is a poet and visual artist living in Chicago. Her writing has appeared in literary journals, including Verum Literary Press and Nine Cloud Journal, and her paintings have exhibited across the country. Playing Time in Tongues, published by Querencia Press, is her first book of poetry.

- Zach Arnett (He/Him) is a magnet tester out of Fort Wayne, IN. His work can/will be found in NOÖ Weekly, Stoked, 90's Meg Ryan and Stone of Madness.

- Zephyr James (they/them) is a fierce advocate with a mushy heart. They offer pieces of themself as a grief & death doula, a consultant, and an academic. They can often be found exploring nature, celebrating queerness in all its forms, or contemplating the human condition in their velvet chaise lounge.

- Zo Copeland is a writer from the South West (UK). They are inspired by their lived experiences of queerness and disability, and by their magical experiences in nature. Zo writes to connect with people, evoke change, and challenge taboo subjects. @zocowrites

OTHER TITLES FROM QUERENCIA

Allison by Marisa Silva-Dunbar
GIRL. by Robin Williams
Retail Park by Samuel Millar
Every Poem a Potion, Every Song a Spell by Stephanie Parent
songs of the blood by Kate MacAlister
Love Me Louder by Tyler Hurula
God is a Woman by TJ McGowan
Learning to Float by Alyson Tait
Fever by Shilo Niziolek
Cutting Apples by Jomé Rain
Girl Bred from the 90s by Olivia Delgado
Wax by Padraig Hogan
When Memory Fades by Faye Alexandra Rose
The Wild Parrots of Marigny by Diane Elayne Dees
Hospital Issued Writing Notebook by Dan Flore III
Knees in the Garden by Christina D Rodriguez
Provocative is a Girl's Name by Mimi Flood
Bad Omens by Jessica Drake-Thomas
Beneath the Light by Laura Lewis-Waters
Ghost Hometowns by Giada Nizzoli
Dreamsoak by Will Russo
the abyss is staring back by nat raum
How Long Your Roots Have Grown by Sophia-Maria Nicolopoulos
The World Eats Butterflies Like You by Isabelle Quilty
Playing Time in Tongues by Vita Lerman
unloving the knife by Lilith Kerr
5 Spirits in My Mouth by Pan Morigan
You Shouldn't Worry About the Frogs by Eliza Marley
Now Let's Get Brunch: A Collection of RuPaul's Drag Race Twitter Poetry by Alex Carrigan
The Dissection of a Tiger by Tyler Walter
Reasons Why We're Angry by Sophia Isabella Murray
An Absurd Palate by Alysa Levi-D'Ancona
Stained: an anthology of writing about menstruation Curated by Rachel Neve-Midbar & Jennifer Saunders
Tender is the Body by Alise Versella
House of Filth by Kei Vough Korede
The Beginning of Leaving by Elsa Valmidiano
TASEREDGED (watch out!) by Tommy Wyatt
Dear Nora, by c. michael kinsella
adulteress by Chloe Hanks
Sessions of a Sandstorm by Isaac Miebi Mendez
atrophy by Shilo Niziolek